# HORRIBLE HISTORIES

# ENGLAND

**TERRY DEARY**

ILLUSTRATED BY **MARTIN BROWN**

**■SCHOLASTIC**

For Iain Gibbons – the winner of the *Horrible Histories*
Brainiest Boffin competition, 2003. TD, MB.

Scholastic Children's Books
Euston House, 24 Eversholt Street,
London, NW1 1DB, UK

A division of Scholastic Ltd
London ~ New York ~ Toronto ~ Sydney ~ Auckland
Mexico City ~ New Delhi ~ Hong Kong

First published in this edition by Scholastic Ltd, 2004
This edition published 2009

ISBN 978 1407 11041 7

Page layout services provided by Quadrum Solutions Ltd, Mumbai, India
Printed and bound in the UK by CPI Bookmarque, Croydon, Surrey

10 9 8

# CONTENTS

# Introduction

History is horrible but it is MORE horrible in some places than others. Some places have all the luck ... the BAD luck. And England is one of them. England has had cruel kings and mean queens, rotten raiders and woeful wars, terrible tortures and evil executions.

Oh, yes, other parts of the world have had all these things – but England has had them all packed into a small space.

AND the poor English have had to suffer the rain as well! The English went out and conquered a quarter of the Earth just to escape the rain. They always went for the hot places – Australia, Africa, India.

But here's the funny thing about the English ... many of them like to take a bit of their Englishness with them wherever they go. All around the world these sad people build English pubs and serve 'Full English Breakfasts' in the morning and 'Fish and Chips' for lunch or dinner (or both). Some of them don't seem to trust 'foreign' people, which is a bit odd. ALL the people in England were 'foreign' at one time.

And here's another funny thing. Saint George wasn't even English. So why did the English pick him for their saint?

5

Er ... no, he wasn't. Someone should tell these English people the TRUTH. The truth with all the horrible bits left in. What we need is a 'Horrible' history of England.

# Barmy Britons

There was no such place as 'England' till the Angles invaded around 1,600 years ago and made it 'Angle-land' or England. In fact the place probably didn't even have a name except 'Home' to the first people to arrive there.

So, before we come to the history of 'England' we need a quick history-of-the-place-that-would-later-become-England.

### Early timeline

**500,000 BC** Almost-human apes walk into England when it's still joined to Europe. These old apes have since been called *Homo erectus* by scientists. They (the ape-men, not the scientists) hunt hippos and mammoths and use sharp sticks as spears. They can still be seen in schools where they are called history teachers.

**225,000 BC** Smarter apes called Neanderthals move in and by 130,000 BC are killing giant elephants and hippos in the area we now call the Thames. But...

**34,000 BC** Really really clever humans called *Homo sapiens* come along and the old Neanderthals have had it. But...

**16,000 BC** An ice age drives out even the clever humans – who unfortunately aren't clever enough to invent double glazing and central heating for their caves.

**10,000 BC** It's warm again and those clever humans are back. By around 6500 BC the ice has melted and the sea has risen. Britain's an island. Poor Europe is cut off!

**2800 BC** Stone-age humans start work on Stonehenge monument. It's either a temple for sun worship or a set of giant's cricket stumps. Who knows?

**2750 BC** The 'Beaker People' – who bury their dead together with pottery drinking cups or 'beakers' – arrive from Germany and start settling. No one stops them. (Not to be confused with Adolf Hitler who tried to arrive from there about 4,700 years later.)

**750 BC** The cut-throat Celts are coming. It's a popular place and it could get more crowded than Blackpool beach on a sunny summer Sunday. But don't worry. The Celts will soon be pushed out to Wales, Cornwall, Scotland and Ireland.

**300 BC** The Celtic 'La Tene' people are sacrificing humans to their gods. But being English they do it in a very sporting way … they smash your skull before they finish you off.

**55 BC** Roman Julius Caesar lands. He came, he saw – he went back home to Rome.

**54 BC** Caesar's back. But it's too much trouble to conquer the Britons in the south of England. So he leaves again.

AD **43** Emperor Claudius arrives and the cut-throat Celts are driven north and west. This time the rotten Romans want to stay in the south and east.

AD **60** The Britons in England revolt. They are led by Queen Boudica. She burns down the temple for 'god' Claudius and massacres every helpless Roman she can find. But the Romans win through in the end. Boudica poisons herself (maybe).

AD **122** Romans STILL in England. Emperor Hadrian even builds a wall all the way across the middle of Britain to keep the Scots out – two million tons and 140 km of rock and soil to keep out the killer Celts in kilts. (Note: In the twenty-first century it no longer works.)

AD **212** And here come the Saxons, the Jutes and those Angles who will give the south of Britain its new name – Angle-land (that's England to you and me). At first they are just pirates raiding the south coast.

AD **367** Now those savage Scots and plundering Picts come down from the north *as well as* Saxon pirates from the east. B-I-G trouble. Worst of all, some of the northern attackers – the Attacotti – are said to be cannibals.

AD **408** The Saxon attacks get stronger in the south as the Roman

9

forces rush off home to help defend their home city against barbarians. In 409 the Romans go home.

AD **450-ish** The most powerful Brit leader is Vortigern. He invites the Angle tribe leaders Hengist and Horsa over from Germany to help fight the Saxons. Big mistake. Hengist and Horsa's Germans decide to stay.

AD **500-ish** King Arthur leads the Celtic Britons in a fight against the Angles and Saxons. But in 539 he is killed by his own nephew Mordred. The story may be just a legend, but the Britons are certainly fighting among themselves and that lets the Saxons win. As Arthur probably never existed it's no surprise he lost. Barmy Brits believe he's sleeping and will be back when Britain is in danger.

AD 793 The Vikings arrive. They massacre, rob and soon they'll settle too. Where's Arthur when you need him? Still sleeping?

AD 798 The Saxons aren't too bothered by the odd Viking raid … yet. So they split England into little kingdoms and go on fighting each other, just as the Britons did. And look what happened to them! King Ceowulf of Mercia (the Midlands) attacks King Edbert of Kent. Ed is captured and Ceowulf has the Kent king's eyes put out and his hands cut off.

10

AD **865** The Vikings land an army and the north and east of England become Viking land. In fact the greedy turnips (well, Swedes actually) would take over the whole of England but for…

AD **878** Alfred the Great fights back and says, 'You Vikings keep the north and east – you can even call it Danelaw. My Saxons will keep the south and west. We'll call it Wessex.' And they had a deal.

AD **1066** The Normans arrive from France and still Arthur doesn't show. That must be one deep sleep.

*Did you know…?*
In 1984 a digger came across a mummified corpse in a Cheshire bog at Lindow. Tests showed he'd been dead over 2,000 years. He'd been killed pretty horribly…

Cruel kids may like to visit 'Lindow Man' at the British Museum in London. At least you can see the top half. The digging machine sliced him in two. The bottom half is still stored in a museum cupboard.

11

## Dreadful days

The poor English people don't get enough holidays – except for teachers who, as we know, get too many. (At least that's what putrid parents say when really they want rid of you from under their feet.)

The Irish get St Patrick's Day (17 March) off school and work, to wear shamrock and remember their favourite saint (even though Patrick was Welsh).

The Americans have Thanksgiving Day (fourth Thursday in November) to massacre a lot of turkeys and remember when the Pilgrim Fathers landed in America. (Not that the Pilgrim Fathers had any turkeys to terminate.)

The French have Bastille Day (14 July) to remember murdering a few posh people at a prison.

But do the English get St George's Day off?

No, those poor people don't. So in this book there are another dozen days (one a month) for the English to find excuses to skive. Here's the first...

**23 APR** **Dreadful Diary Day 1**
*23 April – St George's Day OR Shakespeare's Birthday*

Three reasons to have a street party on 23 April...
• it is St George's Day
• it was the day Shakespeare was born
• and also the day he died – which must have made his birthday party go a bit flat.

Who was this St George?

Well, the English prefer the old folk story of George and the dragon...

*HORRIBLE HISTORIES* NOTE*:*
This must be read in a very sweet voice so your little brothers or sisters don't get too tewwibly fwightened.

Once upon a time, in a faraway land, there was a big, nasty dragon. It had sharp claws and huge teeth and a skin like old green leather. But worst of all it had poisoned breath, as deadly and smelly as the boys' toilets in your school.

The big nasty dragon lived in a cave on the hillside close to a city. When it grew hungry it lashed its tail and knocked down houses and scared all the people in the city below. But don't feel too sorry for the people in the city – they were pretty wicked people. Little did they know ... the dragon was their punishment.

The only way the king of the city could keep the dragon happy was to feed it two live sheep every day. The king went out to the flocks on the hillside and spoke to them. He said, 'I want two sheep.' Then he pointed. 'I'll have ewe and ewe.'

After a year there were no sheep left. So the king had to feed people to the dragon to keep it quiet. Of course no one wanted to go and be the dragon's dinner. The king had a lottery and the loser had to go instead of a sheep. As the king drew the lucky number he said, 'Who are ewe today?'

But one day his daughter, the prettiest princess in the palace, said, 'It's me, Daddy! I've won!' (She was very pretty but she was also stupid.) The king sighed and cried as the princess was led to the hillside and left to be a monster's munch.

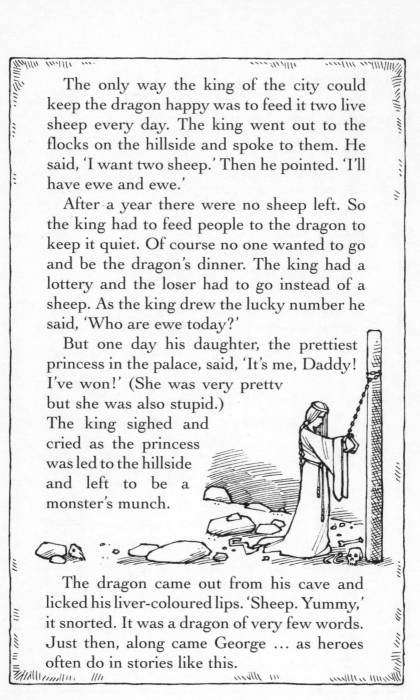

The dragon came out from his cave and licked his liver-coloured lips. 'Sheep. Yummy,' it snorted. It was a dragon of very few words. Just then, along came George ... as heroes often do in stories like this.

First he stabbed the dragon with his lance, then he took the belt from the princess's dress and wrapped it round the dragon's neck. George led the wounded dragon down the hill to the city. If the monster stopped or stumbled George would grasp the belt and 'drag on' it.

'I have captured your dragon,' he told the cheering people.

'Kill the bleeding thing then!' someone shouted.

'Yeah, it's bleeding all over my doorstep,' a woman screeched.

'No,' George said. 'You have been very wicked people and the dragon is your punishment. If you all promise to become Christians THEN I will kill the beast.'

'Oh, all right,' the people agreed.

So George killed the dragon – which was not offered the choice of becoming a Christian – and everyone lived happily ever after.

Except the sheep, of course.

One writer, called Edward Gibbon, said this saint was George of Cappadocia (now Turkey). (You probably know there's a monkey called a gibbon – the writer must have been one of them because he tried telling the English that George was a real villain and NOT a saint.)

Gibbon said that George of Cappadocia…

• was a crook who sold rotten bacon to the Roman army

A SAINT'S GOTTA MAKE A LIVING SOMEHOW

• was made bishop of Alexandria by the Roman Emperor and ruled with awful cruelty
• used Roman troops as bully boys to stay in power
• was finally seized by the people of Alexandria and hanged

Not a nice man to have as your 'saint'.

## By George!

Amaze your teacher with these St George facts.

• George was supposed to have crossed from Ireland to Wales in order to visit England. Today the choppy sea he crossed is known as St George's Channel. Being a saint he probably wasn't sea-sick.

I GUESS THERE'S NO SUCH THING AS HOLY VOMIT

• The Christian Crusaders fought at the battle of Antioch (Turkey) in 1098. St George turned up to help them. (Or so they said.) He became the saint of Christian knights and they wore his badge – a red cross on a white background – for luck.

- King Henry V of England called on St George to help in the Battle of Agincourt (France) in 1415. Henry won and the English were given a holiday and a feast day on 23 April. Help from saints is cheating a bit. But...
- In 1538 King Henry VIII said people were NOT allowed to worship St George – Henry said that was the sort of thing his enemies the Catholics did. But the ordinary people still had parties. It was still a good excuse to get drunk.
- In the 1600s George was back – Charles II and James II chose St George's Day for their coronations. But the next king, William of Orange, was Dutch so St George's Day was ignored again.
- England has been ruled by six King Georges. The last one had a medal made for bravery and called it 'The George Cross'. It was named after the king but the picture on the cross shows the saint. Very confusing.
- St George is an important saint in Catalonia, Portugal, Genoa, Venice, Albania and Greece as well as England. He must be kept pretty busy with all those people praying to him.
- He is also the saint of knights and archers – pray to him if you want an arrow escape. St George is also the saint of boy scouts.

- In the twenty-first century there were attempts to make 23 April a St George's Day holiday for all of England. Birmingham led the way with street entertainment and parties.

*Horrible Histories* **Ancient royal jest**

King Edward VI, son of horrible Henry VIII, hated the idea of saints…

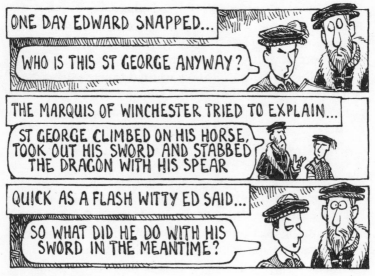

Funny eh?

Oh, all right, maybe not.

**23 APR**

**Celebrate this day:**

Join the boy scouts and slay some dragons…

…OR join some dragons and slay some boy scouts.

But if you're not impressed by gorgeous George, you could celebrate Shakespeare instead. Go to Stratford-upon-Avon (where Will was born) and light 52 candles on his grave – one for each year of his life.

# Island invaders

England would have been a pleasant place if it wasn't for the horrible humans who lived there. England's not too horribly hot, not too cruelly cold, not too madly mountainous, not too floodingly flat, not too dustily dry or too wash-out wet.

Just right. So lots of people wanted to live there – even if it meant pushing out the ones who got there first. There were always new pushy people ready to invade.

## Rotten Roman Britain

The first b-i-g invasion was by the ruthless Romans of Emperor Claudius in AD 43. Some of the Brits loved being ruled by the Romans and enjoyed Roman ways. They learned Latin and took to togas, they thought baths were brilliant and made beasts of themselves at banquets. But the Brits who rebelled were vicious in their vengeance. A Roman writer, Tacitus, wrote about the fighting in AD 58…

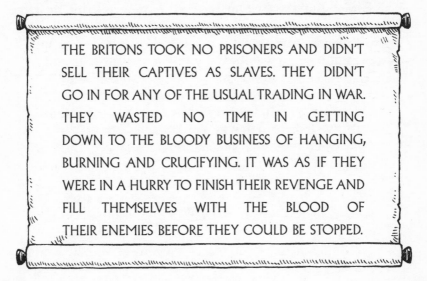

THE BRITONS TOOK NO PRISONERS AND DIDN'T SELL THEIR CAPTIVES AS SLAVES. THEY DIDN'T GO IN FOR ANY OF THE USUAL TRADING IN WAR. THEY WASTED NO TIME IN GETTING DOWN TO THE BLOODY BUSINESS OF HANGING, BURNING AND CRUCIFYING. IT WAS AS IF THEY WERE IN A HURRY TO FINISH THEIR REVENGE AND FILL THEMSELVES WITH THE BLOOD OF THEIR ENEMIES BEFORE THEY COULD BE STOPPED.

## Big bad Boudica

The biggest Brit rebellion was led by Queen Boudica. She rampaged round the country and massacred people in Colchester and St Albans and then killed 70,000 in London. The English Channel was said to be purple with Roman blood. (That would make paddling in the sea at Dover a bit messy.)

At last she came up against the little Roman army of Suetonius Paulinus. She had 250,000 and it looked like a walkover. But the Brits parked their ox-carts with their food and tents and families and set off on a wild charge. The Romans drove them back and the Brits couldn't escape because the ox-carts formed a wall. Dead Brits fell among dead oxen as they were slaughtered. 80,000 Brits died but only 400 Romans. (At least that's what the Romans said!)

Queen Boudica died of shock – or maybe she poisoned herself. We'll never know for certain.

Now you'd think the Romans would be happy. But one Roman general, Poenius Postumius, had refused to join the fight against Boudica. He was chicken.

After the battle Poenius Postumius was so ashamed. What did he do? Killed himself. Quick clean poison like Boudica?

No. Much messier. He placed a sword to his belly and fell on it.

20

*HORRIBLE HISTORIES* NOTE:
Don't try this at home. It makes a real mess on the carpet and your parents don't have servants to clear up after you the way the Romans did.

AND TO THINK...THEY SAID HE HAD NO GUTS!

### Nice to eat you
The Attacotti tribe, who attacked the Romans in England around 367, were accused of being cannibals and eating their victims. They came from the area where Glasgow now is.

A Roman complained...

A VICIOUS TRIBE OF CALEDONIA, THE ATTACOTTI, DELIGHT IN THE TASTE OF HUMAN FLESH. WHEN THEY HUNT THE WOODS FOR PREY, IT IS SAID THAT THEY ATTACK THE SHEPHERD RATHER THAN HIS FLOCK OF SHEEP. ODDLY, THEY SELECT THE BRAIN PARTS, BOTH OF MALES AND FEMALES, WHICH THEY PREPARE FOR THEIR HORRID MEALS.

The report could be a lie, of course. But it gives us a nice picture of a tribe that set out on a sheep raid...

**Quick question:**
How did the Picts and Scots get past Hadrian's wall?
**a)** They made big ladders.
**b)** They built leather hot-air balloons and floated over.
**c)** They paid the Roman guards to let them in.

*Answer:*
**c)** The Scots bribed the guards.

## Days and ways of death

History books will often tell you how people such as the Saxons lived. The *Horrible Histories'* job is to tell you how they *died*. Here are a few foul ways...

### Pain and plague – AD 664
If the battles and the assassins didn't get you then the dreadful diseases would. In 664 there was a plague that swept through England and it killed the Archbishop of Canterbury.

The history-writing monk, Bede, explained WHY England was bothered by these plagues...

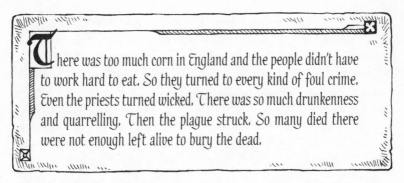

There was too much corn in England and the people didn't have to work hard to eat. So they turned to every kind of foul crime. Even the priests turned wicked. There was so much drunkenness and quarrelling. Then the plague struck. So many died there were not enough left alive to bury the dead.

Bede sounds a bit like your teacher, doesn't he? 'Work *hard* and you'll be too *busy* to get into trouble.'

### Drought and dads – AD 682
If the diseases and the wars didn't get you then the drought and starvation would – with a bit of help from your dad.

In 682 a terrible drought shrivelled the crops and left the Saxons of the south of England starving. They ate all the cows and sheep and chickens and pigs. Then they started on some of the things you wouldn't eat. The dogs...

Then they started on the cats and even the rats. Finally the parents started eating the children. You'll be pleased to know it did them no good. The adults starved and to end their misery they jumped off the cliffs to their death. Serves the deadly dads right. And it wasn't just dads...

### Stabbing and stepmothers – AD 978
Those Saxons loved squabbling among themselves. No wonder they had trouble keeping the Vikings and the Normans out! They were too busy fighting each other.

23

Take young King Edward, for example. He was king of England. But his stepmother – just like the wicked stepmother in 'Cinderella' – wanted him out of the way. She wanted to grab all the glory for her own child – like the Ugly Sisters.

It's *said* that she invited King Edward to stay at Corfe Castle in Dorset to do a bit of hunting, but it was Edward who was hunted. He arrived back at Corfe and the trap was sprung. A servant offered him a cup of wine to cool him down.

His body was rescued from the well and people went to see it. The bones gave them miracle cures. Dead Ed was made a saint – even though he'd been a bad-tempered bully when he was alive!

Stepbrother Ethelred became king.

Wicked stepmother? Went into a convent for the rest of her life as a way of showing how sorry she was.

**15 MAR** **Dreadful Diary Day 2**
*15 March – Ides of March OR Caesar's Liberation Day*

An unlucky day in the Roman calendar. And the day, in 44 BC, on which Roman leader Julius Caesar was murdered ... by the Romans who should have been his friends!

In England, there should be a holiday on this day to celebrate the death of this savage Caesar who dared to invade.

He didn't do it once, he did it twice! Caesar made a mess of it in 55 BC. He admitted it. He decided to land his soldiers on the beaches. But the ships were not built to get close enough to shore.

Then Caesar told the famous story of the standard bearer of the tenth legion...

NO ONE WANTED TO BE THE FIRST TO JUMP INTO THE WATER AND FACE THE BARBARIAN BRITISH. THEN ONE BRAVE MAN, THE STANDARD-CARRIER OF THE TENTH LEGION, JUMPED INTO THE WATER CARRYING THE STANDARD. THE GREATEST DISGRACE A ROMAN SOLDIER CAN SUFFER IS TO LET YOUR LEGION'S STANDARD BE

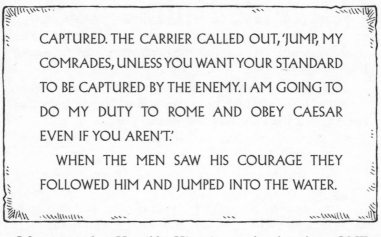

CAPTURED. THE CARRIER CALLED OUT, 'JUMP, MY COMRADES, UNLESS YOU WANT YOUR STANDARD TO BE CAPTURED BY THE ENEMY. I AM GOING TO DO MY DUTY TO ROME AND OBEY CAESAR EVEN IF YOU AREN'T.'

WHEN THE MEN SAW HIS COURAGE THEY FOLLOWED HIM AND JUMPED INTO THE WATER.

Of course the *Horrible Histories* reader has just ONE question to ask...

We'll never know. Caesar was unlucky when he invaded Britain – both times. Storms wrecked his ships – both times. After the second invasion he went away and didn't go back – 23 daggers on 15 March made sure he never could.

**15 MAR** **Celebrate this day:**
Go to the south coast and stroll along the beaches looking for Roman invaders. Arm yourself with an ice-cream and a bag of chips.

# Miserable Middle Ages

The Normans arrived and many of the English became their slaves. Norman lords, English workers.

As if that wasn't bad enough, there were famines and fighting to kill you, terrible taxes and terribler tortures to make you suffer, dreadful diseases and rowdy rebellions to bring pain to peasants and lords alike. (But more to the peasants.)

## Middle Ages timeline

**1066** The nasty Normans arrive. 1,500,000 English are ruled by just 20,000 Normans. They rule by terror and by building castles. The king owns all the land and shares it out among his barons. Only ONE of these barons is English – the rest are Norman French. What happened to the English? They became peasant workers.

**1120** Norman King Henry I loses his only two sons, William and Richard. Very careless. Sons were in the 'White Ship' crossing to France. The crew of the ship were probably drunk. They certainly ended in the drink. The White Ship hit a rock and went white to the bottom. Henry has no male heirs now.

**1135** Henry I dies and his daughter Matilda starts a war against his nephew Stephen. As usual, when the English start fighting each other, someone tries to invade them. This time it's the sneaky Scots (in 1138). The Scots are defeated. Phew!

**1153** Another Norman invasion! This time Henry Plantagenet lands with his army and Stephen says, 'Tell you what. Let's not fight. You let me stay as king and I promise you can be king when I die.' Henry agrees and Stephen very kindly dies the following year. Henry becomes Henry II. The Plantagenets rule and will do so for over 300 years.

**1215** King John upsets everyone in sight – the barons, the Pope, the people. In the end they force him to sign the Great Charter (Magna Carta in Latin). It gives some power to the people. John then says, 'I may have signed it but I am going to ignore it!' But John very kindly dies. (Or was he poisoned?) The French invade *again* but are defeated at Lincoln. They do keep trying, don't they?

**1264** Simon de Montfort from France (where else?) starts 'The Barons' War' against King Henry III. De Montfort is killed at the Battle of Evesham and his head is sent to Lady Mortimer, the wife of his enemy. But the foul French troublemaker has set up a 'parliament' (French for 'a place for talking') where the people get to tell the king what to do. It's still around 740 years later. Thanks, Simon.

28

**1272** Edward I becomes king and sets about turning England into 'Britain'. He batters the Welsh and he hammers the Scots. This all costs a lot of money which means a lot of taxes for the English peasants. They are not happy.

**1337** Edward III says, 'I'm King of France.' Philip VI of France says, 'Oh, no you're not.' Edward invades France, which makes a nice change, and starts a war that will last 116 years and cost a lot of poor peasants more taxes. They won't like that.

**1348** The 'Black Death' plague arrives in England and will kill a third of the English people – but mainly the poor. If you get huge purple blisters and start spitting blood then it's bad news. Say goodbye.

**1381** The Peasants' Revolt. A 'Poll' Tax causes the trouble. (I said they wouldn't like it.) It's a tax on every 'head' (which is what 'poll' means) – and as most people have a head, most people have to pay it. Led by Wat Tyler, the peasants march on London to see the king, lopping off a few lordly heads along the way.

**1399** Henry IV takes the throne from Richard II. The English are fighting among themselves again. These scraps will be known as 'The Wars of the Roses'. Remember they're STILL trying to fight the Hundred Years War that began in 1337. So...

**1453** French King Charles VII nips in and wins the Hundred Years War while the English are fighting each other. Typical. Finally…

**1485** The Battle of Bosworth. King Richard III loses the last big battle of the Wars of Roses and it's the end of those Normans and Plantagenets. It's a Welsh family, the Tudors, who will take over for the next hundred years or so. Terrible Tudors.

## Mean Middle Ages monarchs

England has had its fair share of cruel kings and mean queens. The worst were in the Middle Ages…

### John (1167–1216)

There have been lots of legends about John but this one is probably horribly true…

King John threw all Jews in prison and tortured many of them till he was paid 60,000 silver marks by their fearful families. It wasn't enough. In 1210 John arrested all wealthy Jews and demanded a ransom of 1,000 marks each for their release.

Roger of Wendover told the story of a 'Jew of Bristol' who refused to pay his ransom. The king ordered his torturers to pull out one of his molar teeth – the big teeth at the back of the mouth with deep roots – every day until he paid the 1,000 marks. He stood it for seven days, but paid the ransom when they started on his eighth tooth.

### Henry III (1207–1272)

A baron from the de Maurisco family of Lundy Island (Devon) plotted to kill Henry. De Maurisco's punishment was to be executed at the Tower of London by being hung, drawn and quartered. But first he was dragged to the tower tied to a horse's tail. Painful.

In 1265, at Flimwell in Sussex, Henry III's cook got into an argument with local villagers. They killed him. Henry's revenge was horrible. He picked 300 people from the village, took them into a field and had them beheaded.

### Edward I (1239–1307)

In 1290, Edward I sent secret orders to all Jews. They were to leave England by 1 November along with their wives, children and goods. The order said they would suffer no injury, harm or damage as they left, but the punishment for any Jew who stayed behind after that was death.

By October (a month before the deadline) 16,000 had left for France and Belgium, but many did not arrive. The meanest trick was this...

### Henry IV (1366–1413)

Henry IV faced a rebel army led by Harry Hotspur. They met in a bloody battle at Shrewsbury (Shropshire) where 20,000 rebels were slaughtered and Harry Hotspur got an arrow in the face.

Harry was taken off to Whitchurch (down the road) where he was buried.

But Horrible Henry wasn't happy. He wanted the world to see what happened to his enemies. So he had Harry dug

up, and his corpse stuck on a spear and put on show in Shrewsbury. But Henry STILL wasn't happy. So the crumbling corpse was cut up and bits were sent all round England – a leg here, an arm there … and there.

Hacked Harry Hotspur. Horrible Henry.

### Miserable monks

Life in old England was tough. But some people made it even tougher for themselves by becoming monks. They worked and prayed and lived in cold stone cells and slept on hard beds. In return they expected a nice, warm, cosy place in heaven after they died. All those old monks suffered, but some suffered more than others.

### 1 Famous father

The Venerable Bede lived in the north-east of England (AD 673–735) and is known as the 'father of English history' – so we can blame him for the boring history lessons we've all had to suffer. Bede wrote the first history book about the English people.

There was a story (told after Bede's death) about a miracle that happened when he was an old man.

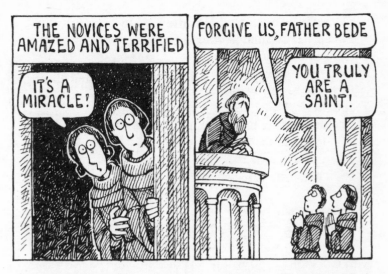

As Bede lay dying a year later, he still insisted on finishing the book he was working on. A young monk took down the words as Bede said them. 'Now it is finished,' the young monk said.

'You have spoken true. It is finished,' Bede said quietly ... then died. What a way to go. A true English hero.

A bit like you finishing your last SATs test then dropping down dead.

## 2 Miracle man

Dunstan (AD 924–988) made Glastonbury in Somerset one of the most famous monasteries in the world. Stories even went around that Jesus had visited Glastonbury and that King Arthur was buried there.

A cup was used to catch Christ's blood as he died on the cross and that cup became known as the 'Holy Grail'. That's supposed to be buried at Glastonbury too.

All nonsense, but good stories like that meant lots of visitors and lots of money for the chief monk Dunstan to build a fine monastery.

Dunstan was a bit odd. It was said he...
- talked to invisible people
- argued with dead people
- saw the Devil in the shape of a dog or a bear or a fox
- fought the Devil and pinched his nose with a pair of tongs
- saw Glastonbury re-built in a dream when he was a boy – then did it as a man.

### 3 Burned brother

Aelred of Rievaulx (North Yorkshire) lived in the 1100s. When Aelred was a boy he said, 'The evil Bishop of York will die soon!' And would you believe it? He was right.[1]

Aelred left his comfortable life in Scotland for a tough life in the Yorkshire monastery. He made things even harder by sitting in a cold tank of water every day. It was SO tough that one of the monks threw Aelred on a fire for being 'lazy'. As Aelred was dying, he said, 'I forgive that monk who threw me on the fire.'

The English can be horribly forgiving.

### 4 A slice of Bacon

Roger Bacon (1214–1294) was a monk too. Monks live in cells, of course, but poor Roger spent a lot of his time in a *prison* cell. He said clever things like 'A rainbow is made when water bends light.' However, the Church said, 'A rainbow is made by God! Lock him up!'

After ten years he was released and carried on with his experiments.

Some didn't work – he tried turning lead into gold. No chance. He also tried an old Chinese recipe to make an

1 The problem with this story is that the Bishop of York at that time was actually quite a good man! Aelred was right about the death, wrong about the evil. Just goes to show, even a saint can't be right all the time.

exploding dust – and *that* worked. He had brought 'gunpowder' to England. Now people could stuff it into bullets and bombs and kill millions of others. They're still doing it. Thanks, Rog.

He tried to create a drink that would make you live for ever. He died, so it didn't work ... which is just as well because if all these old history characters were still alive the world would be very crowded.

## 5 Agony abbot

Horrible Henry VIII got rid of the monasteries, nicked their treasures and pulled down the buildings. He also had many of the top monks executed.

In 1539 the abbot of Glastonbury monastery was Richard Whiting. He was questioned in the Tower of London for months, then taken 130 miles back to Glastonbury with two of his loyal monks to be executed.

The exhausted old man was fastened to a wooden board and dragged behind a horse to the abbey.

First the monks were hanged, then they were beheaded and their heads were stuck on poles over the gateway to the abbey. The message was plain for all to see... 'You don't mess with Henry.'

**14 OCT** **Dreadful Diary Day 3**
*14 October – Hastings Day OR William's Day*
The year 1066 is supposed to be the most important date in English history. On 14 October that year William the Conqueror met and beat King Harold of England at the Battle of Hastings. It changed English history for ever. But nobody bothers to take a holiday to remember that date. It's time they did.

You don't need reminding of the story of that day, do you?

You do? Oh, very well, but it's so well known you can only have *just enough* to remind you, not the whole lot.

Here it is with some important words missing. Replace the numbers with the correct words.

Clues? You don't need clues? Oh, very well. There are 12 missing words – here are 13. ONE is NOT in the passage below … but it COULD be.

Confused? Good.

**Clue words:**
head, legs, beard, bones, arrow, bum, arms, neck, naughty bits, throne, gun, hair, eye

The trouble started with King Edward the Confessor. He was King of England and he promised his (1) to William of Normandy. He knew Harold, (9) man of England, had his (8) on it and wanted his (10) on it.

Mind you, Harold himself had promised the (1) to William. Harold went across to Normandy and put his hand on a box of (2) from Saint Rasyphus and Saint Ravennus. Harold said, 'The (1) is all yours, William.'

But Edward died at the end of 1065 and Harold grabbed his (1).

William was furious. And the Pope was on William's side. 'Go and invade England with my blessing. And here is a ring with the (3) of Saint Peter for luck.'

William started to build ships and gather an army to attack. But, before he could, Harold faced another invader: the Viking Harald Hardrada – and, as you know, Hardrada means 'tough-talking'.

Hardrada was one of those Vikings who got himself into a wild state before a Battle and fought like an animal– the Vikings called them 'berserkers'. He had long (3) and a thick (4).

Harold hurried to Stamford Bridge in Yorkshire to meet Hardrada in battle. It was Hardrada who ended with an axe in the (5). One of his berserker friends held the bridge till an English soldier floated under it and stuck a spear up his (10).

Meanwhile William had landed at Hastings. He jumped from the ship and looked a bit of a plonker when he fell forward up to his (6) in water. (That must have washed the (3) of St Peter in the ring.) But crafty William grabbed a handful of sand, turned to his men and said, 'See how I've seized English land already?'

On 13 October 1066 Harold arrived and the battle began the next day. Harold sat on a hilltop and watched the Normans struggle to get up on tired (7). William wore the (2) of Saint Rasyphus and Saint Ravennus around his neck for luck. But every (12) seemed to fall short. (A (11) would have been useful but it hadn't been invented.)

But William ordered the archers to fire higher and one struck Harold in the (8). The Normans rushed forward and hacked wounded Harold to the ground. They stripped him and cut off his (7) and (6). Finally they lopped off his (9) with a chop to the (5).

The battle was over and William was the one to get his (10) on the English (1). And that's life – (3) today and (11) tomorrow.

Celebrate this day:
Go to Hastings and practise your archery OR go
berserk in Yorkshire.

**14 OCT**

*Answers*:
1 = throne, 2 = bones, 3 = hair, 4 = beard, 5 = neck, 6
= arms, 7 = legs, 8 = eye, 9 = head, 10 = bum, 11 =
gun, 12 = arrow
Odd word out = naughty bits. But it COULD have
been in the story. When Harold was hacked to pieces
one of William's knights cut off Harold's naughty bits.
William was furious and sent the knight back to
Normandy in disgrace. 'You don't treat a noble enemy
like that, *mon ami*,' William said.

# Creepy country

England was said to be the most haunted country in the world. Full of creepy castles, haunted houses, spooky cellars and headless horsemen. It seemed you couldn't turn a corner without hearing phantom footsteps following you in the fog.

What went wrong? Well, in May 2003 scientists told the world...

THERE ARE NO SUCH THINGS AS GHOSTS

Yet some people *still* believe in the supernatural. So maybe the scientists are wrong! In that case, where will you find ectoplasm in England? Here is a typical terrible tale that might just be true...

## Hylton Castle, Tyne and Wear

In the Middle Ages, Lord Hylton of Hylton Castle in Sunderland caught a stable lad, Robin Skelton, asleep. He took a horse whip and beat and kicked the boy to teach him a lesson. But he killed him – so the boy didn't get much chance to learn from his mistake.

AND IF I CATCH YOU NAPPING AGAIN YOU'LL *REALLY* BE IN TROUBLE

Lord Hylton tried to cover up his crime by throwing the boy's corpse into the castle pond. The ghostly boy rose from the pond and to this day he can be heard moaning, 'I'm ca'ad! So ca'ad.' (That's 'cold' to you posh people.)

He may even be heard singing a pathetic little song…
Why not join him? Here are the words…

**The Ca'ad lad's lament**
I worked in the stable but I fell asleep.
His lordship found me dozing in a big straw heap.
He whipped me and he kicked me till he made me weep,
Then he chucked me into the pond so deep.

*Chorus:*
*I'm ca'ad, I'm ca'ad, I'm so ca'ad,*
*I'm slimy and clammy as a lump of lard.*
*If you work for Hylton be on your guard,*
*He hits you with a whip and he hits you hard.*

My sad, sad tale is not a fable.
I was a groom in the Hylton stable.
I worked just as hard as I was able … of course.
Alas I never said goodbye to Mabel … the horse.

*Chorus*

If you go to Hylton then you'll be thrilled.
Go along there when the night air's stilled.
Old Hylton he did beat me till I was killed.
Listen hard and hear me moan, 'I'm chilled!'

*Chorus*

**What happened next?**
Lord Hylton was sent for trial on the charge of murdering Robin Skelton, but the judge was an old friend of his.

They say a ghost can only rest when it has had 'justice' – when the killer has been found and punished. Poor Robin never got his justice and that's why he can never rest in peace.

Horrible fact: Robin's haunt, Hylton Castle, is vandalized more than any other ancient monument in Britain.

## The Hampton Court ghost

If England is the most haunted country in the world then Hampton Court Palace near London is one of the most haunted houses. Apart from a couple of Henry VIII's queens (who pop up everywhere) there is also the curious case of Elizabeth I's nurse, Sibell Penn. This is her terrible tale…

Sibell nursed Elizabeth when the princess caught smallpox

YOU'LL SOON BE WELL

TA, SIB-BELL

Elizabeth got better but Sibell caught the disease and died

OH, POO!

BOO HOO!

Sibell was buried in Hampton Church with a fine marble statue

VERY FINE

WHINE WHINE

But in 1829 the tomb was smashed and her bones scattered

Hampton Court has a famous maze. Imagine being lost in there with Sibell! Try it.

45

## A-maze-ing fun

If you can't get along to see Sibell yourself then try this
ghostly game with a friend – or, if you haven't any friends,
try it with an enemy.

*You need:*
• a pencil • a watch • a pen • two lumps of ice
• a map of Hampton Court maze

Where will you get that map? Funny you should ask.
Here, is the answer. Trace it.

*To play:*
1 Place your pencil at the opening near the bottom.
2 That's where you are, being chased by the ghost of
Sibell. If you get to the centre, you are saved. If you fail,
she gets you. You have just 20 seconds start.
3 Start the watch.
4 Find your way to the centre before the 20 seconds
are up.
5 If you fail you have the spine-chilling punishment – a
lump of ice down the back of your neck.
6 Now switch with your friend/enemy. They start at the
centre and have just 20 seconds to find their way OUT to
save themselves – or get the ice cube if they fail.
The coolest game you'll ever play.

## Wake the dead

How did English people come to believe in vampires –
creatures that could rise from the dead? Here's a
curious explanation…

WE OFTEN RUN OUT OF SPACE IN THE GRAVEYARDS FOR NEW BODIES. THEN WE DIG UP THE OLD COFFINS TO MAKE ROOM

FOR EVERY 100 COFFINS WE DIG UP WE FIND AROUND FOUR HAVE SCRATCH MARKS ON THE INSIDE OF THE LID. SO THOSE FOUR HAVE BEEN BURIED ALIVE AND HAVE WOKEN INSIDE THEIR COFFINS

TO SAVE THEM FROM THIS WE LAY THE CORPSE ON A TABLE AT HOME FOR A FEW DAYS. WE HAVE A PARTY WHILE WE SEE IF HE'LL WAKE. WE CALL THE PARTY A 'WAKE' IF HE'S STILL DEAD AFTER THE 'WAKE' WE BURY HIM. HE'S DEAD…

UNLESS, OF COURSE, HE'S A VAMPIRE!

Some people asked to be buried with a rope around their wrist that went through a hole in the coffin lid and was fastened to a bell. If they woke inside the coffin they could ring for help!

### Chills in the churchyard

In 1674 some boys were on their way home from school and took a short cut through the graveyard in Basingstoke (Hampshire). They heard the most gruesome sound of all ... tapping coming from one of the graves.

The grave was Mrs Blunden's and she was freshly buried. She'd taken too much poppy-water for a headache and knocked herself out. The doctor had said, 'She's dead,' and they'd buried her.

Then she woke up and started knocking on her coffin lid till the boys heard her. By the time her coffin was opened her body was bruised with the struggle – but this time she really was dead.

Knock, knock! Who's there? Shudder! Shudder who? Shudder stuck to aspirin.

### Dreadful Diary Day 4

*6 January – Twelfth Night OR Werewolf Day*

You need a day off to take down the Christmas decorations – it's the 'twelfth night' after Christmas day, you see? Shakespeare wrote the play *Twelfth Night* to be performed on this evening – but the play has nothing to do with Christmas.

But for real horrible excitement you need to know that 6 January is the day when werewolves roam about – especially when it is a full moon that day! So, even if Potty Parliament won't make this a holiday you MUST tell your parents…

Werewolves are humans who turn into wolves when the wolfbane flower blooms. Not EVIL people – ANY people can do it.

If your parents don't believe you, tell them…

Now some of our scaredy-cat readers may be wetting themselves when they read this. Don't. You see it is easy to spot a werewolf. Tell your friends how to do it – with the help of *Horrible Histories* you could even give a classroom talk!

*Did you know…?*

King John of England was accused of being a werewolf. After he was dead some monks said they heard his body moving in its grave. That must mean he could not rest in holy ground, they thought! So they dug up his body and buried it outside the churchyard.

**Celebrate this day:**

Take a day off school, sit in front of a nice warm fire and read a *Horrible Histories* book – armed with a silver bullet and a box of chocolates. OR dig up a dead king.

# Batty beliefs and curious customs

Tourists go to England to see some of the country's curious old customs. They go to Buckingham Palace to see 'The Changing of the Guard', for example.

Some of the curious customs have died out along with the batty beliefs. Others still go on – though most people don't know why!

## Curious customs
### 1 May baths
In May the weather got warmer. After a winter of wrapping up in thick clothes the English finally threw them off and had a bath.

The man of the house had the first dip while the water was fresh. Then the woman, then the children and finally the babies. By then the water was so dirty you could lose a baby in it! It could be why there is the old English saying...

## 2 June weddings

The people of England usually got married in May or June. Why? Here is a curious answer.

I GOT MARRIED IN JUNE BECAUSE I STILL SMELL QUITE FRESH AFTER MY BATH IN MAY

And the bride carried a bunch of flowers to drive away any putrid pongs that were left over. They still do ... carry flowers, that is.

## 3 Valentine dreams

Girls only. Place a bay leaf under your pillow on Valentine's Night (14 February). You will dream. In the dream you will see who loves you. This may NOT be a good thing, of course.

AAAA AAA

## 4 Shrove silliness

On Shrove Tuesday English people eat pancakes and act silly. (It's not the pancakes that send you silly, of course.) Many places have curious customs like...

**Pancake races** – women running down the street like their knickers are on fire and tossing pancakes.

**Village football** – where two teams battle to capture a ball and take it back to their village – no other rules and lots of broken legs.

**Rope pulling** – like tug-of-war but with a stream between the teams. The losers get wet and muddy. (Much more fun.) Go to Ludlow for that.

**Tiptoeing** – at Gittisham in Devon the children simply tip-toe from house to house begging for money. You can pay them if you are daft enough, or tell them to...

TIPTOE TA-TA!

### 5 Hare-meat pie

In Hallaton (Leicestershire) in 1770 a woman was chased by a mad bull. Just as it was about to gore her a hare ran between them. The bull was confused and the woman was saved. She gave a piece of land to the local church as a 'thank-you' present. (I suppose she thought God sent the hare to save her.)

She said, 'Each year the church must have a contest between Hallaton village and Medbourne village. There will be three barrels and the teams try to kick the barrels over the village borders.'

That sounds fair enough. BUT the prize is a pie made from the meat of two hares.

YOU SAVE SOMEONE FROM A HORRIBLE DEATH BY RISKING YOUR OWN LIFE AND WHAT'S YOUR REWARD? THEY KILL YOU AND EAT YOU

These days the pies are made of beef.

### 6 Dead deer days

Twice a year (late July and December) the king or queen gives four dead deer to the Lord Mayor of London. Why?

It all started with Dick Whittington – and if you haven't heard his story go to the pantomime some time. Mayor Whittington was a rich bloke who loaned King Henry V some money to fight in France (the Hundred Years War).

Henry V won a great victory at the Battle of Agincourt, then came home…

And it's gone on every year since.

### 7 Grim gurning

Every year since 1267 there's been a fair at Egremont in Cumbria – on the third Sunday in September. The good news is there are roast apples to eat, and, for fun, people climb a greasy pole to get a leg of lamb. But most weird is the 'gurning' contest.

To take part you put your head through a horse collar and pull as ugly a face as you can. The ugliest wins.

Try this ancient game at school.

### 8 Coffin custom

In 1595 a Hertford farmer, Matthew Wall, was being carried to his funeral when the coffin was dropped. Ooops! The clatter woke the farmer up and he knocked on the coffin lid. He lived on for many more years.

The old man left £1 for the church to have an annual service in his memory at Braughing Church. On 2 October each year children sweep the lane with brooms – maybe in case any bits dropped off him when the coffin was dropped?

All of which has nothing to do with the ancient *Horrible Histories* joke:

A funeral was climbing a steep hill when the coffin slid off the back of the cart. It began to slide down the muddy hill, faster and faster. As it passed the chemist shop the lid creaked open and the corpse sat up. He looked at the chemist and begged...

### 9 Blackberry hell

English men, women and children should pick blackberries on 10 October each year and on no other day. According to some, the devil was thrown out of heaven by the angel St Michael and landed in a blackberry bush. As a result, the devil spits on all blackberries – except on this day, which is St Michael's Day.

### 10 Horrible Hallowe'en

On Hallowe'en many children enjoy dressing up and pretending to be ghosts who have slipped through the 'curtain' from the world of the dead. They then call at houses and threaten the owners with a haunting if they aren't given a gift – this is called 'trick or treat' in the United States. Hallowe'en parties are older than the American custom though.

The Celtic people of ancient Britain held a feast to celebrate the end of summer. The Romans said that the British priests (the Druids) made human sacrifices to the gods at the celebration. They claimed the sacrifices were made by fastening prisoners in a huge wooden cage then setting fire to it.

It's probable that the Romans were lying.

*Did you know...?*
A Chinese woman who moved to England had never heard of Hallowe'en or the 'trick or treat' game. She really believed there was a ghost at her door. She threw a pan of boiling water over the eight-year-old boy. Only his mask and bin-liner costume saved him from serious injury. The poor woman was ordered to pay the boy £750 for the scalds he received. Some trick – some treat!

**Rich witch – Eleanor Cobham, Duchess of Gloucester**
In kids' books 'witches' are monstrous hags that fly round on broomsticks and want to roast little Hansels and Gretels alive.

In history books they are ordinary men and women who were clever with herbs and known in their villages as 'Cunning Men' or 'Wise Women'.

Eleanor Cobham simply wanted to be top woman in England. And she didn't care how she got there. She was quite happy to use witchcraft, it was said...

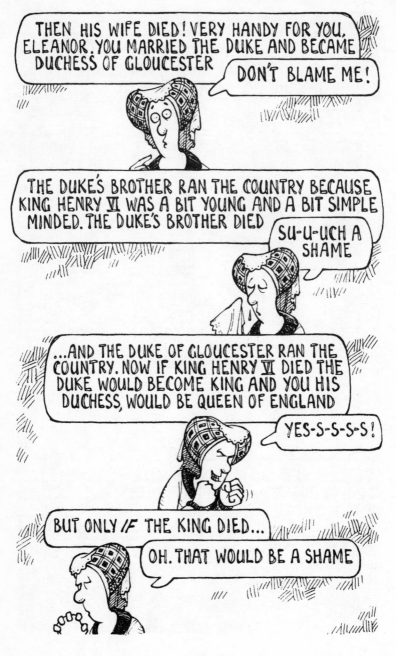

60

**24 JUN** **Dreadful Diary Day 5**
*24 June – Midsummer Day*
Everyone needs a holiday on this day because they'll have been up so late the night before.

On Midsummer Eve (Ghost-watch Night) you should be out and about...

On Midsummer Eve you can also try this old recipe…

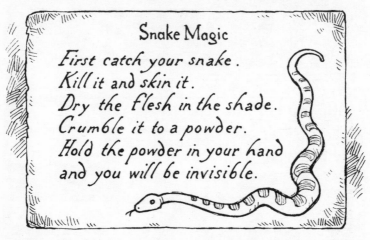

Snake Magic

First catch your snake.
Kill it and skin it.
Dry the flesh in the shade.
Crumble it to a powder.
Hold the powder in your hand
and you will be invisible.

So, maybe you don't NEED a day's holiday from school on Midsummer Day!

This snake powder nonsense sounds silly – the sort of thing simple peasants might have believed in the Middle Ages. But that recipe was written in the days of Charles II, just 350 years ago.

**Celebrate this day:**

**24 JUN**

Grind up your mummy…

…OR go out and trick-or-treat in your local churchyard.

# The revolting English

The English have always been revolting. If they didn't like their rulers then what did they do? Go on strike? Give their lordships a good talking to? Sulk?

No. They rioted. Some riots turned more serious and ended up as revolts. From Boudica[1] (the queen who massacred a few Romans and lost) to today's football supporters (who get upset if England lose a game).

The English are still rioting. For example, 1 May each year – May Day – is a popular time to march through the streets and throw rubbish bins through shop windows.

In 2003, schoolchildren joined in too. They skived off school, marched through the streets of English towns, shouted rude things about the Prime Minister and generally had a lot of harmless fun.

Why? Because they said they didn't want Britain to go to war in Iraq.

Did these skivers make any difference? No. Britain went to war in Iraq anyway.

Typical. MOST of the revolting English ended up losing. They never learned from history.

### The 1381 Peasants' Revolt

In 1377 King Edward III needed money and lots of it.

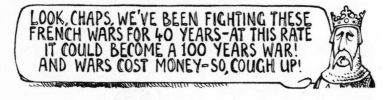

LOOK, CHAPS, WE'VE BEEN FIGHTING THESE FRENCH WARS FOR 40 YEARS—AT THIS RATE IT COULD BECOME A 100 YEARS WAR! AND WARS COST MONEY—SO, COUGH UP!

---

1 Yes, all right, Boudica was 'British' not 'English'. But she lived in the place we now call England, so let's just give her a mention.

Edward then died and his young grandson Richard II came to the throne and tried the same tax in 1381. But when the collectors came around this time they discovered there were a lot of people 'missing' as families tried to dodge paying the tax.

When the king sent in tax collectors to check on the cheats there was trouble. Rebels set off for London, led by protesting peasant Wat Tyler, looking for tax collectors, bishops and lords to lop off their heads. The rebels also had it in for lawyers.

One man who saw the lawyers panic and run said...

*It was marvellous to see how even the most aged and frail of them scrambled off, as nimble as rats or evil spirits.*

The rebels wanted to destroy the riches of the posh people, not steal them. But it didn't all go quite to plan.

**Five revolting 1381 facts**
1 One group of peasants set a London house on fire and came across some barrels.

If they'd only looked inside they'd have seen the barrels were full of…

They died.

**2** Another band of 30 men found a wine cellar and drank as much as they could. They set fire to the cellar – but were too drunk to escape. They died too.

**3** The rebels took a dislike to Flemish weavers in London because they believed they took work from English weavers. They set out to massacre as many as possible. They had a simple test.

The Flemish people made it sound more like 'brote und kase'.

If they failed the test they were brutally murdered on the spot. Thirty-five were found in one street, taken out into the road and beheaded.

So, next time someone offers to take your photograph and tells you, 'Say cheese,' remember this *Horrible Histories* advice: DON'T.

**4** Simon Sudbury was the Archbishop of Canterbury and one of the main targets of the rebels. He was hiding in the Tower of London when the rebels came to get him. He tried to slip out at the Tower's watergate but a woman spotted him and he was captured.

Of course the rebels wanted him beheaded – but they weren't very good at it. It took eight chops to get the head off – one of the chops was followed by Sudbury calling out, 'This is the hand of God.' (Actually it was the hand of a clumsy peasant, but no doubt God put Sudbury right when they met a few chops later.)

The archbishop's scarlet cap was nailed on to his head and the head was stuck on a pole over London Bridge. The clumsy axeman was cursed (it is said) by going blind and mad.

NOT FAIR... HE LOST HIS MIND BUT I LOST MY WHOLE HEAD

5 When Wat Tyler finally got to meet the king the meeting took place out of sight of his peasant army. One of the king's men called to Wat…

*Tyler, you're the greatest thief and robber in the whole of Kent.*

Wat drew his dagger and rode towards the king. That was the excuse that Mayor Walworth of London needed to draw his own dagger and stab Wat. The king's squire, Ralph Standis, joined in and ran his sword through the rebel several times.

Somehow Wat staggered back to his horse and his friends took him to a house to care for him. But the king's men dragged him out and chopped off his head. (He may already have been dead by then, of course.)

Wat Tyler had been murdered, and no one else wanted his risky job. The peasants gave up and went home. End of The Peasants' Revolt.

*Did you know…?*

The march gave rise to a nasty little folk song – well, nasty if you're a bird-lover, that is.

The 'king' of the birds is the wren. So when the rebels sang of killing 'the wren' in a song called 'The Cutty Wren' they really meant killing 'the king'. But they weren't just going to kill him! Here's a bit of the very long song:

*Oh how will you cut him up?*
*said Milder to Moulder*
*With knives and with forks,*
*said John the Red Nose.*
*Oh that will not do,*
*said Milder to Moulder*
*Great hatchets and cleavers,*
*said John the Red Nose.*

*Oh how will you boil him?*
*said Milder to Moulder*
*In pots and in kettles,*
*said John the Red Nose*
*Oh that will not do,*
*said Milder to Moulder*
*Great pans and large cauldrons,*
*said John the Red Nose.*

*Oh who'll get the spare ribs?*
*said Milder to Moulder*
*We'll give 'em all to the poor,*
*said John the Red Nose.*

71

So the plan was to kill the king-wren, cook him and share the flesh out among the poor. Yummy.

And the story gets even nastier. Catching and killing wrens was an old English custom since before Roman times. On the day after Christmas, peasants believed they had the freedom of the kingdom. On that day they netted and killed wrens for luck. It's only in the past 100 years or so that this cruel custom has died out.

A tasty wren may have been better than the food they had to eat. Thomas Walsingham, a writer at the time of the Peasants' Revolt, said...

*The poor were left to eat the rotting flesh of animals that had died from disease.*

## Rotten rebels

There were many riots and rebellions after the 1381 Peasants' Revolt, of course. Here are a few horrible highlights...

### 1450 Jack Cade's Rebellion in Kent

Having started the Peasants' Revolt in 1381, the Men of Kent started it off again. This time they were led by an Irish murderer, Jack Cade.

Again they wanted tax cuts, again they marched on London and again they beheaded the Archbishop of Canterbury. It was a dangerous job in those days.

*Funny fact*

King Henry VI's 'Treasurer' (who collected the taxes) was also beheaded. His head was placed on a pole opposite the head of the Archbishop so they were 'kissing' each other.

The lords promised to give Cade what he wanted so his army of peasants went back to work on the land. Then, of course, the king ordered Cade's arrest.

Typical. Never trust a kunning king.

*Foul fact*
Cade was hurt when he was arrested, and he soon died. But that didn't stop the lords hanging his body, cutting his guts out and burning them, beheading the body and cutting it into quarters.

The other leaders suffered the same fate and the bits of their bodies were sent around England as a warning to others. Horrible.

## 1549 Kett's Rebellion in Norfolk
Peasants had always survived by having 'common' land that everyone in their village shared. They could keep a cow there for milk or a few sheep for wool.

Then greedy rich lords started grabbing the common land, 'enclosing' it behind fences and keeping the peasants off. This was to cause trouble for 100s of years to come.

In Wymondham, Norfolk, Robert Kett led a riot which involved tearing down the hedges and fences that made the enclosures. It turned into a full-scale rebellion as he gathered an army and attacked Norwich.

*Funny fact*
The worried leaders of Norwich went out to meet Kett and ask for peace. They were met by a boy who dropped his trousers and showed them his backside.

WHAT DID HE SAY?

DUNNO. SOUNDED LIKE 'PFFFTT!'

Kett's army had just one cannon and managed to set fire to Norwich's 'Cow Tower'. (The gunner must have scored a bull's eye ... geddit? Bull's... Oh, never mind.)

Then his men marched forward and hammered at the doors of Norwich's town walls. They wanted to know if they could come in and buy some food as they'd had no breakfast. The people of Norwich said, 'You must be joking!'

So old Robert captured Norwich and held it for a month.

*Foul fact*

When Kett was finally defeated, 49 of his men were hanged instantly. They had to climb a ladder with a rope around their necks. The ladder would be taken away and they'd be left to swing. In Norwich that day so many were hanged the ladder was wrecked.

Kett was arrested and sent to hang from the walls of the city. The order said his body had to hang there...

...until he should fall down on his own.

In other words, till his body rotted. Horrible.

The enclosures went on.

## 1607 The Captain Pouch Rising in the Midlands

The problem of 'enclosure' was still annoying the poor people of England 50 years after Robert Kett's rebellion.

Trouble broke out next in the Midlands, and this time the leader was John Reynolds. John was nicknamed Captain Pouch and a report of the time explained...

> *He is given the name Pouch because of a great leather pouch which he wears by his side. In this pouch, he swears to his followers, he holds the power to defend them against all their enemies.*

*Funny fact*

When Reynolds was caught and the pouch was opened, what was found inside?

**a)** a piece of mouldy cheese
**b)** a fortune in gold
**c)** a book of magic spells

OR MAYBE A FORTUNE IN MAGIC CHEESE

*Answer:*
**a)** A piece of green cheese was all they found. Maybe it was so mouldy its smell could have gassed the enemy – a bit like your dad's socks.

*Foul fact*

Pouch's army were armed with sticks and stones. Gentlemen with swords rode through them and hacked them down killing 40 or 50. Three of Pouch's followers were hanged and quartered. The government promised to make life better for the revolting peasants, but they broke their promises.

The enclosures went on.

**5 NOV** **Dreadful Diary Day 6**
*5 November – Good Guy Day OR Glorious Day*
This day used to be a holiday to celebrate the capture of Guy Fawkes. Good old Guy was only trying to blow up parliament when the slimy Stuart King James I was in there.

**Quick test your teacher:**
Question: On what date was Guy Fawkes arrested?

*Answer:* 4 November. That's right. He was caught BEFORE midnight of 5 November.

Of course Guy thought he was doing everyone a favour – he didn't think he was a terrorist, he thought he was a freedom fighter. Everyone knows what happened to him.

Guy Fawkes was taken in front of King James (who was wearing his night clothes). The king was said to be frightened.

Guy refused to betray his friends. He was tortured by being stretched on a rack but still he refused to talk. By 9 November Guy's friends had been captured and killed. It was only then that he talked.

On 30 January 1606, nearly three months after he was arrested, Guy Fawkes was taken to be hanged, have his guts cut out and burned, then have his head cut off and his body chopped into quarters.

Everybody knows that, but here are five foul and fantastic facts to flummox or fascinate your friends.

# Five facts for the fifth...

### 1 Party time

In January 1606 (before Guy Fawkes and the plotters had been tried and executed) Parliament passed a new law. It said that 5 November would become a holiday of public thanksgiving. People lit bonfires to celebrate and threw dummies on the fire which were dressed as Guy Fawkes. The first record of this is at Cliffe Hill in London where the Pope joined Guy Fawkes in the flames.

### 2 Barrel-load of fun

Within a few years of the plot people began to use fireworks on 5 November and still do to this day. In Lewes in Sussex there is a 5 November tradition for setting fire to barrels of tar and rolling them down a hillside. This is extremely dangerous, of course, and the adults find it such hot, thirsty work they have to go to a local pub to drink and cool off. Or at least that's their excuse! As a little boy of Lewes wrote in 1822...

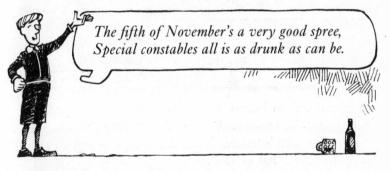

*The fifth of November's a very good spree,*
*Special constables all is as drunk as can be.*

### 3 Scotton damp squibs

For many years the people of Scotton village in Yorkshire refused to celebrate 5 November with fireworks and bonfires. This village was where Guy Fawkes used to live and the people didn't think it was fair that Guy should take all the blame.

### Four Unlucky 13s and Lucky Fives

There were just five plotters who set out with a plan to blow up Parliament. As 5 November grew closer they brought in more people to help. The last man, Francis Tresham, was number 13.

No sooner had Tresham joined than things started to go wrong. A warning letter ended up in King James's hands, Guy Fawkes was caught and the plotters were captured or killed.

Some historians believe Tresham was 'planted' by Parliament to catch the plotters. Reports later said Tresham was taken to the Tower of London for questioning and that he died there. Three doctors said that he died of an illness. Some historians believe that he died under torture.

But one historian has a fantastic theory about the 13th man. He believes Tresham escaped! The idea is that Tresham had done such a good job for the king that the government arranged Tresham's escape. A woman came to visit Tresham and brought female clothes – the guards were changed and *two* women walked out ... one of them was Tresham in disguise. Very unlikely, but if it's true then he was *lucky* 13!

BUT ... if 13 was unlucky for the plotters, King James had a thing about the number Five. The Gowrie Plot in Scotland was an earlier attempt to kill James. It had taken place on a Tuesday, the fifth of the month. The Gunpowder Plot took place on the fifth ... and again it was a Tuesday! James said this proved...

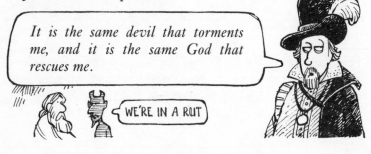

*It is the same devil that torments me, and it is the same God that rescues me.*

WE'RE IN A RUT

## 5 Ghostly Guy the Phantom Fawkes

Guy Fawkes was questioned in a room in 'The King's House' of the Tower. This 'house' was built in Henry VIII's reign for the Tower's governor to live in. King Henry's second wife, Anne Boleyn, spent her last night in that room before going to her execution the next morning.

For many years after the Gunpowder Plot soldiers swore that Guy Fawkes haunted that room.

**5 NOV**

**Celebrate this day:**
Build a bonfire and burn a dummy of King James I for a change, OR march to your local firework display with a banner saying, 'Guy Fawkes was innocent!'

# Terrible Tudors and slimy Stuarts

The Miserable Middle ages were pretty ... well, miserable. As the poor peasants waved goodbye to them they must have thought...

GOOD RIDDANCE

Little did they know there was WORSE to come! The terrible Tudors and the slimy Stuarts brought torture and execution for people who didn't follow the monarch's religion. And that was tricky because the monarchs kept swapping between Catholic and Protestant – and some of them like Henry VIII and James II and Charles II were BOTH! If you didn't swap quickly enough you could be tortured or hanged or burned at the stake.

COME BACK! PLEASE! WE LOVED YOU!

## Terrible timeline

**1509** Horrible Henry VIII comes to the throne. He is one of the Welsh Tudors, of course. The English haven't had a lot of English kings, have they?

**1534** Henry doesn't like being told what to do by the head of the Catholic Church, the Pope. Henry

WAIT! THERE'S SOMETHING WRITTEN ON THE CROWN 'FOREIGN FOREHEADS FOREVER'

wants a divorce – Pope says, 'No.' Henry says, 'Right! I'll make my own Church of England and give myself a divorce.' This new 'Protestant' religion will cause untold misery in its struggle against the old Catholic Church. And English will kill and torture English, of course.

**1588** English Catholics get the help of the Spanish who send a huge fleet of ships – the Armada – to invade England. Good old English weather and some sharp English seamen see them off.

**1603** Elizabeth I is dying and just before she pops her clogs she says the next king should be James VI of Scotland. He comes down to London and becomes James I of England. The poor English will never get to rule themselves.

**1605** Catholics plot to blow up King James in his Parliament. Plotter Guy Fawkes is caught the night before, tortured and executed.

**1642** King Charles I and the posh 'Cavaliers' get into a Civil War against the English Parliament and their supporters, the 'Roundheads'. Charlie the chump loses and the Roundheads have him executed in 1649. Roundheads make the king a no-head. England ruled by Oliver Cromwell – an Englishman! But not for long…

81

**1658** Cromwell dies. The English invite chopped Charlie's son, Charles II, to take his dad's throne. Cromwell's body is dug up, cut up and thrown in the River Thames while his head is stuck on a pole at Westminster Hall for 25 years.

**1665** The plague is back – 70,000 die in London alone. Then, a year later, the Great Fire of London destroys a lot of the filthy slums that give homes to the rats that spread the plague. The Lord Mayor of London, Sir Thomas Bloodworth, hears about the fire but doesn't quite realize how bad it is.

**1688** James II (like grandad James I) has trouble on 5 November. This time it's William of Orange landing with an army at Torbay. The English don't want Catholic James II any more so the lords have invited William over. It's called 'The Glorious Revolution', and not-so-glorious James runs away to France. The English have got rid of the Scottish Stuarts and now the country is run by a Dutchman.

**1707** England has shared its Parliament with Wales since 1536 (when a Welsh Tudor was ruling). Now, a 100 years after having a Scottish king, it finally gets around to sharing its Parliament with the old enemy, Scotland. At last we have 'Britain'. But Britain won't be 'Great' until 1801 when Ireland joins.

82

## Elizabeth I (1533–1603)

In 1561 the English sailor John Hawkins attacks a Portuguese ship carrying African slaves. Does he set them free? No he sells them and makes a nice fat profit.

So, in 1564 Queen Elizabeth decides she wants a slice of this business. She gives Hawkins money to buy and sell more slaves. Hawkins makes a profit again and Good Queen Bess gets a good queenly cut.

Miserable for the slaves, but it will pay for another jewel-encrusted dress for the mean queen. (Or it will pay for the £80,000 worth of food her palace ate in a single year.)

That's how Elizabeth started the English slave trade that would bring over 200 years of grief.

Liz needed lots of good sailors and ships to keep her rich. In 1563 she had a law passed that meant a lot more Englishmen would become sailors. Guess what that cunning law said. Was it...?

a) *Every man in England must learn how to swim and be tested by being thrown off a bridge once a year.*

b) *Every man in England must give wood, nails or sails to help build one thousand new ships.*

c) *No person in England can eat meat on a Wednesday, Friday and Sunday.*

What happened if you were caught eating meat on a Wednesday, Friday or Saturday? You could go to prison for three months. A London woman served meat in her tavern and spent a painful day in the pillory.

### What she didn't do...
The Spanish were about to attack England. So Lizzy met her troops and told them what a tough Tudor nut she was and how they would beat the Armada. She said...

*I know I have the body but of a weak and feeble woman; but I have the heart and stomach of a king, and of a king of England too.*

The trouble is that speech was written AFTER she was dead. She did speak, but she did not say those exact words.

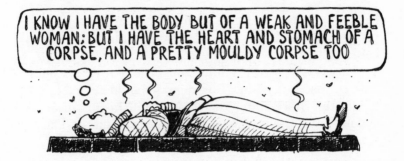

*Did you know…?*

The Armada wasn't quite the end of the Spanish invaders. Seven years later in 1595 the Spanish landed at Penzance in Cornwall … with just four ships and 400 men.

They set fire to houses and cut a local squire in half with a cannon-ball. The cannon-ball ended up stuck in the wall of his house and it was left there for years afterwards!

When the Spanish invaders knew a big English army was coming they jumped back on their ships and sailed back home.

As the severed squire might have said…

**Test your Stuart teacher**

The Stuarts were as horrible as any other English ruling family. Charles I (1600–1649) became the only English king to be executed by the people. Did he deserve it?

Well, he was a great big snob. He thought he was a 'god'. He ordered that…

- people who served him had to do it kneeling down
- when he was standing up no one else was allowed to sit down.

He thought he could rule without the parliament of the people and went to war with the people. He lost, of course. (The War and his head.)

Teachers know everything and history teachers know MORE than everything. So teachers should get ten out of ten for this quick slimy Stuart quiz while history teachers should get 11 out of ten. Just answer 'True or False?' about the following. Easy-peasy.

1 If you were a gentlemen you could keep pigeons in dovecotes in your garden. *The birds were kept to carry your messages.* TRUE/FALSE?

2 If you played village football then you could be part of a team of up to 1,000-a-side and the goals may be three miles apart.

fig.1
a penalty

There were hardly any rules and riots or murders could happen during a game. *King James banned the playing of sports on a Sunday.* TRUE/FALSE?

3 James had a new Bible published in 1611. Before that you had to use the Geneva Bible. *This Bible was nicknamed the Breeches Bible because it said Adam and Eve 'sewed fig leaves together and made themselves breeches'.* TRUE/FALSE?

**4** You would go to bed with nightcaps on because there were so many draughts. *Doctors said there had to be holes in the top of the nightcap to stop the brain from overheating.* TRUE/FALSE?

**5** You were advised to clean your teeth with powdered stone. *This removed the stains from your teeth.* TRUE/FALSE?

**6** You could go to school in Stuart times, if your parents could afford it. *Teachers were highly respected in the times of King James.* TRUE/FALSE?

**7** Elizabeth I had shown how clever women could be. *King James followed her example and believed that girls should be educated as well as boys.* TRUE/FALSE?

**8** Breakfast was a very important meal for Stuart families. *Your breakfast would usually be a boiled egg and a glass of water.* TRUE/FALSE?

**9** If you were lucky (and a boy) you might be taught a business by a master craftsman. You would become his apprentice. However, apprentices had to live by strict rules ... including one that said *you had to have your hair cut.* TRUE/FALSE?

**10** As a Stuart person you are a bit superstitious. So... *If you saw a woman walking backwards then it was a sure sign she was a witch.* TRUE/FALSE?

*Answers*:

**1 False**. Pigeons and doves were kept to be killed and eaten.

**2 False**. James wrote a book in which he encouraged people to play sports on a Sunday ... after they had been to church.

**3 True**. For most families the Geneva Bible was the only book they ever owned.

**4 True**. But, while they wore nightcaps on their heads they didn't usually wear nightdresses or pyjamas.

**5 True**. Unfortunately it also removed the enamel from the teeth and allowed them to rot quicker. So did the mouth-washes made with honey.

**6 False**. Many pupils admired their teachers but other adults didn't. Teachers were very badly paid (even though they worked from 7 a.m. till 5 p.m.) and had few holidays. Some had to take other jobs in order to make a living – William Swetman, for example, was also a fishmonger.

**7 False**. James was set against schools for girls. He said educating women was like taming foxes – the only effect is to make them more cunning.

**8 False**. Breakfast was usually a slice of bread, washed down with a drink of beer. River water was usually too unhealthy to drink. But even people who had really fresh water believed it was bad for your health.

**9 True**. Apprentices who grew their hair too long could be arrested, have a basin forced over their head and have the hair below the basin sliced off. They could also be sent to prison for this! Girls could become apprentices to hat-makers and dressmakers but usually trained as servants.

**10 True**. That's what the superstitious people of James's time believed.

## Uncivil war

The English have spent a lot of time fighting French and Scots and ... other English. (Fighting your own people is called civil war.)

The Civil War of the 1640s ended when Charles I had his head lopped because he argued with Parliament. The king's men (the Cavaliers) fought on against the armies of Parliament (the Roundheads). But there were other horrible history moments in that war that hurt just as much as hacking Charlie's head...

### The big bang

At Torrington (Devon) the king's army needed somewhere to store their gunpowder. They stored it in the church. All 50 barrels of it. In February 1646 they were defeated by the Roundheads and held prisoner in the church – along with their gunpowder.

One day there was a huge explosion – bits of church and bits of prisoner rained down in a torrent on Torrington.

Who lit it?

Did the prisoners blow themselves up? Or was it an accident? We'll never know because the bright spark who set it off didn't live to tell the tale.

## Dropped and chopped

Royalist prisoner Dr Hudson tried to escape from Woodcroft house in Cambridgeshire. He climbed over the wall and hung on, ready to drop into the moat. But a guard caught him and chopped through his wrists. Another guard fished him out of the moat and beat him senseless. Then he cut out the doctor's tongue. Dr Hudson died but the soldier kept the tongue for many years. He said it was for luck.

## Fresh flesh

The Roundheads were 'Puritans' who hated the way the Church of England people worshipped. In the Church of England the people ate bread and wine and believed it changed into the flesh and blood of Jesus in their mouths.

Some Roundheads captured an old Church of England woman, Agnes Griffin, in Rugby. They decided to give her a *real* taste of flesh and blood. It is said they:

• crucified her on a tree
• cut her down and forced her to drink her own blood
• forced her to eat her own flesh

The woman recovered. The local judges gave her four shillings (20p) to pay for the way she had suffered.

**Bolton blood**

In 1644 the Earl of Derby attacked the Roundhead town of Bolton and massacred 1,500 of its people who were trying to surrender. So, when the king lost the war, the Earl was taken back to Bolton to be executed. In the words of the Bible...

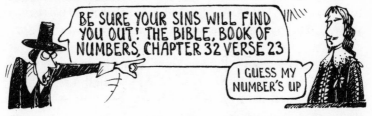

BE SURE YOUR SINS WILL FIND YOU OUT! THE BIBLE, BOOK OF NUMBERS, CHAPTER 32 VERSE 23

I GUESS MY NUMBER'S UP

He spent his last night in a tavern near the execution spot. What was the name of the tavern?

a) The Man and Scythe
b) The Man and Axe
c) The Man and a Rusty But Pretty Sharp Pen Knife

*Answer:*

**a)** It must have been tough looking at that inn sign, knowing that his own head would be scythed off in the morning. Swish.

**Hot horses**

At the Battle of Marston Moor (North Yorkshire) in 1644, Prince Rupert fought for the king. Oliver Cromwell defeated him and sent Rupert's horsemen galloping away for their lives.

They reached a farm where, luckily, the farmer's servant was a great fan of Prince Rupert. She threw open the gate to let the runaway Royalists through. Gutsy girl.

They didn't stop to say thanks. In fact they were in such a hurry they trampled her into the ground. Gutsy girl with guts spread all over the dusty road.

Oooops!

## Woeful women

Women in history have always been given a hard time. In Tudor England it was no better. They suffered the crime of just being women. Not fair.

They suffered more horrible historical punishments too. In King's Lynn, Norfolk, Margaret Day was a servant. In 1531 she poisoned the family she worked for.

A man would have been hanged, but Margaret was sentenced to be boiled alive. She was lowered into boiling water time and again till she died. As she died it is said her heart exploded from her chest and hit the wall of a house opposite. Gruesome.

And women suffered the cruel ducking stool. They were fastened to a chair and lowered into a freezing river over and over again while a crowd jeered at them. This wasn't just to try witches. It was used to punish women for...

• gossiping
• nagging
• getting drunk.

A horrible history for English women, then. But which of these foul female facts are false – and which are true?

**1 A married woman** was punished if she was caught cuddling another man. She could be put in the stocks and whipped and have her hair cut off. (That's true.) A married man who cuddled another woman got NO punishment AT ALL. TRUE/FALSE?

**2 A good wife** was said to be one who got up at 6 a.m. every morning. TRUE/FALSE?

**3 A woman in danger** was a woman near a fire in the Middle Ages. But better fireplaces made women safer. (That's true.) By the 1600s and 1700s their biggest danger was drowning. TRUE/FALSE?

**4 A woman farm worker** was paid the same as a man if she did the same work. TRUE/FALSE?

**5 Women actresses** were allowed on stage in the 1660s and were very popular. (That's true.) In 1706 Mrs Baxter was a great success when she played the part of Lord Foppington. TRUE/FALSE?

**6 A strong woman** (Mrs Alchorne) was put on show by her husband in the 1750s. (That's true.) She lifted a blacksmith's anvil with her teeth. TRUE/FALSE?

**7 A witch** in England would be tied to a wooden stake and burned. TRUE/FALSE?

**8 A poor woman** could be paid to whip dogs out of the church. TRUE/FALSE?

**9 A Catholic woman** could be fined for calling the king or queen nasty names. TRUE/FALSE?

**10 A woman wearing trousers** could be whipped as a punishment. TRUE/FALSE?

*Answers:*

**1 True**. On the other hand, when women took part in riots their husbands could be punished for not keeping them in order. A bit like a pupil breaking a window and their teacher getting the blame. (Nice idea.)

**2 False**. A good wife should get up at 4 a.m. in summer and 5 a.m. in winter. These 'rules' were written in a book telling women how to be a good wife.

**3 True**. Women like Agnes Ellyot of Sussex who went to a water pit at 4 a.m. on a winter morning and fell in. Young girls drowned in wells and ponds fetching water. Dangerous breakfasts.

**4 False**. In Lincolnshire in 1621 men were paid twice as much as women. Even in the twenty-first century there are many cases of women being paid less than men. Unfair.

**5 True**. Women actors were so popular the theatres gave them men's parts to play. A bit of a change from William Shakespeare's days (1564–1616) when all women characters had been acted by boys.

**6 False**. She lifted it with her knee-length hair. Don't try this at home, especially if you wear a wig. The anvil could drop on your cat.

**7 False**. Nine out of ten people accused of being witches were women. If they were found guilty they were hanged. In Scotland and Europe they were burned. Witch would you prefer?

**8 True**. Poor women were also given jobs as road sweepers and paid to clean and decorate the church. Chasing dogs was more fun – unless the dog decided to bite you.

**9 True**. In 1603 a Wiltshire woman called Elizabeth I 'a bloody queen'. Elizabeth died that year and the same woman was back in court for insulting the new King James I. It didn't help when she called her judge a 'blood-sucker'.

**10 True**. A woman in Norwich was whipped in 1629 for dressing as a man. But there were many cases of women dressing as men to fight in wars with their husbands. They also dressed as men to join gangs of smugglers and pirates.

*Did you know…?*

Many men have killed their wives in England's horrible history. Maybe the strangest killer was George Brougham of Combe in Berkshire.

In the 1600s George was walking to market with his wife Martha. He saw a wasp's nest and said, 'Look at this, Martha!'

As she peered into the nest he crept behind her and stuffed her head into the nest. The angry wasps stung her to death. But George told his crime to his new girlfriend. Someone heard his tale. He was arrested and hanged. His body was displayed on a gibbet for all to see. The gibbet is still there – his body is long gone.

**29 MAY** **Dreadful Diary Day 7**

*29 May – Oak Apple Day OR Stuart-on-a-stick Day*
In 1649 Charles I, King of England and Scotland, was executed. (He was Scottish, so if your teacher tells you 'Charles was the only English king to be executed,' you can say, 'Oh, no, he wasn't – he was the only "King of England" to be executed. Not quite the same.')

England managed without a king for 11 years – Oliver Cromwell ruled as 'Protector'. But when old Olly died the English decided they'd have Chopped Charlie's son back as their king.

He was called Charles too, so he became Charles Two. He'd escaped the chop by hiding up an oak tree for a few days when he lost a battle at Worcester in 1651. That's why the Oak Apple became his sign and his great day.

On 29 May 1660 he took the throne and, would you believe it, that was Charlie Two's birthday! He was known as the 'Merry Monarch' because he was a happy chappy.

Of course the people of England were as miserable as ever when the plague hit them in 1665, then the Fire of London in 1666 ... but at least Charlie Two was merry.

So, you have to laugh. In fact on this day everyone should have a holiday and recite Cheerful Charlie's poem...

## You have to laugh

*'It's being cheerful keeps me going,'*
*Charles the Second said.*
*'Me dad was such a misery*
*That they cut off his old head...*

*'Ha! You have to laugh.*

*'And since I've been upon the throne*
*We've had some fun!' he said.*
*'Except in 1665...*
*The plague left thousands dead...*

*'Ha! You have to laugh.'*

*And though the countless thousands*
*Lost their homes in London's Fire;*
*They had their merry monarch here*
*To raise their spirits higher.*

*Ha! They had some laughs.*

**29 MAY** **Celebrate this day:**
Go to Boscombe where Charlie's Oak tree stands, eat apples and laugh, OR climb any oak tree like a squirrel, and act like a nut.

# Cruel criminals

There's an old saying you've probably heard...

AN ENGLISHMAN'S HOME IS HIS CASTLE

It means an English person is safe in their home. No one has the right to enter unless they are asked.

But it's nonsense. People enter other people's homes all the time without being asked. We call them burglars.

### Rotten robbers

In old England it was even worse than today, because the robbers didn't even bother picking your lock or breaking your window. They could just break through the walls made of woven branches and mud (called 'wattle and daub').

There was one horrific case in the Bedfordshire village of Roxton in the Middle Ages. If there'd been a newspaper around then it might have looked like this...

Win up to one whole pound with our Bugle Bingo!!

1 Grote                                        18 Nov 1269

# Bedford Bugle

## ROXTON ROBBED AND RAVAGED

The village of Roxton is today shattered by a savage attack by a robber gang that has left four dead and three seriously injured.

A gang of armed thugs burst through the walls of Ralph Bovetoun's house and robbed it as two girls staying there fled.

The people in the next house were not so lucky. Maude del Forde and Alice Pressade were in bed when the gang broke in. Maude was in her bed when the men came in. She was struck on the head with an axe to stop her screams being heard. Witnesses have described seeing her brains spilling out on to the pillow. Alice died later from the wounds they gave her.

John Cobbler's house was attacked on two sides with window shutters torn down and the door smashed in. The man was taken outside and killed. His wife Alma and daughter Agnes suffered axe wounds to their heads and knife wounds to the chest and arms. Their other daughter managed to hide between a chest and a basket.

Alma Cobbler was able to describe her attackers before she died. They are tax collectors from the local monastery.

The Sheriff of Bedfordshire has told worried villagers that these evil men will be caught and executed.

If an Englishman's home is his castle then it is sometimes a castle of sand.

And housebreaking didn't stop, even when houses began to be made of bricks and cement. The famous highwayman, Dick Turpin, started his criminal career as a housebreaker – one of a gang who kicked down doors and held the house-owners at pistol-point while they robbed them.

## Ruthless Robin Hood

Robin Hood is one of England's most famous heroes. Famous for 'robbing the rich to give to the poor'. An English outlaw, fighting against the cruel Norman lords. But did this hero really exist?

There *was* a Robin Hood who lived in North Yorkshire – part of a family of thugs. In one day he went to court and faced THREE separate charges. Bold Robin...

• built a haystack in the middle of the road
• attacked the wife of Henry Archer and 'drew blood'
• attacked Juliana Horsse and 'drew blood'

Hardly a hero.

And in today's schools they don't tell you the old tales of Robin Hood, do they? Two hundred years ago children heard this story...

Robin slew Guy of Gisborne

*Have at ye!*

Taking out his knife Robin sliced off Guy's gory head

*Tis an ugly job but someone's to do it.*

Then Robin spiked the head on the top of his bow...

And Robin had finished a good day's work

What about the gentle giant, Little John, in the old tales? Not only does he hack off the head of a monk but he kills the monk's little page-boy in cold blood just to stop him being a witness.

Finally, Robin doesn't die a hero's death. He is tricked by a monk who bleeds him to death. As the old song ran...

Cheerful stuff, eh?

## Pitiless pirates

England is part of an island so of course it had a lot of pirates. These weren't jolly jack tars, sailing the seas and swashing their buckles. They were cruel criminals.

In the 1580s, Stephen Heynes was a painfully pitiless pirate. He had a nasty way of torture...

## Sick surgeons

Surgeons needed to know how the human body worked, so they would cut up corpses to dig around and have a look.

The law said they could ONLY use the bodies of criminals who'd been executed. The trouble is there weren't enough to keep the cutters happy. So they started pinching fresh corpses from graveyards in the 1700s and early 1800s.

In Liverpool in 1826 the police found 11 corpses pickled in barrels and ready to be shipped off to the surgeons. (The body-snatchers went to prison for 12 months each.)

The good news is you COULD stop them digging up your granny! Here's how...

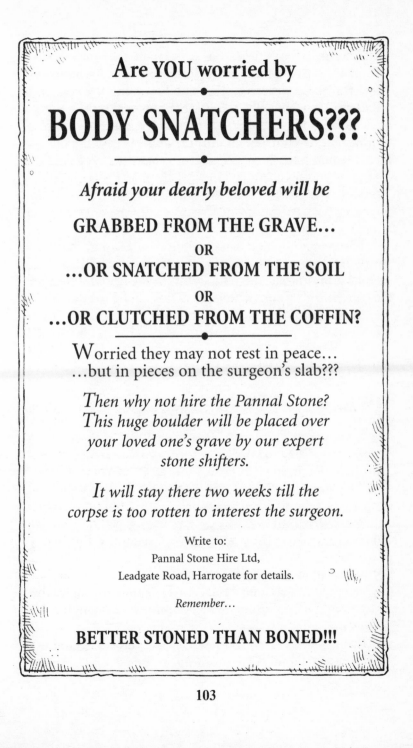

# Are YOU worried by

•

# BODY SNATCHERS???

•

*Afraid your dearly beloved will be*

## GRABBED FROM THE GRAVE...

### OR

## ...OR SNATCHED FROM THE SOIL

### OR

## ...OR CLUTCHED FROM THE COFFIN?

•

Worried they may not rest in peace...
...but in pieces on the surgeon's slab???

*Then why not hire the Pannal Stone?
This huge boulder will be placed over
your loved one's grave by our expert
stone shifters.*

*It will stay there two weeks till the
corpse is too rotten to interest the surgeon.*

Write to:
Pannal Stone Hire Ltd,
Leadgate Road, Harrogate for details.

*Remember...*

## BETTER STONED THAN BONED!!!

The Pannal Stone can still be seen in the graveyard at Pannal. At Woodplumpton in Lancashire there is a boulder too. But it isn't there to keep the body-snatchers out. It's there to keep Meg Shelton IN. She was said to be a witch. Meg could not rest after death and clawed her way out … three times. So the fourth time they put the boulder on top.

It would have been easier just to bury her face down.

## Savage surgeon

Doctor Richard Smith of Bristol went a bit further than most surgeons on Friday 13 April, 1821.

John Horwood had been executed for the murder of his girlfriend (Eliza Balsum). Horwood was just 18 years old. Doctor Smith had the body taken to his hospital to carve it up while young doctors watched and learned. Sick-minded Smith then got a copy of the book written about Horwood's crime. He had the book covered in Horwood's skin. Creepy.

The book is still in the Bristol Record Office.

## *Did you know…?*

In 1649 Anne Greene was hanged for murder in Oxford. Her body was cut down, then kicked and jumped on to make sure she was dead. She was carried off to the surgeon, Dr Petty.

The surgeon thought the body was quite warm for a corpse so instead of cutting her he cured her.

Anne recovered and was set free – after all, the sentence was to hang and she'd done that! She lived to a good old age.

## Smashing smugglers

At Marsden Bay, South Tyneside, a smuggler called John the Jibber betrayed his gang to the tax collectors. The collectors set a trap one stormy night.

But the smugglers defeated the tax men and took their revenge on John. Next morning he was found hanging over the cliff edge on a rope. His eyes had been pecked out by gulls.

John still haunts Marsden Bay…

## Slippery Stuart crime

If you lived in Stuart times could you survive without an honest job? Here are some tricks of the criminal's trade from the 1590s and 1600s to help you. Why not become…

### A whipjack - a beggar with a sad story

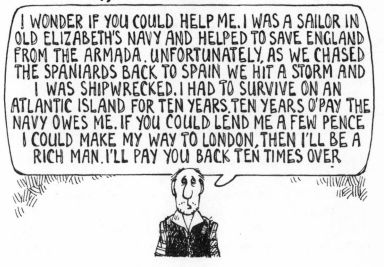

Of course, you are not a shipwrecked sailor, and you'll never see your victim again. Or try simply acting potty...

## An Abraham man – a beggar who talks madly

GOODBYE. WHAT? THANK YOU. THEY SAY I'M MAD. I'M NOT! WELL, NOT VERY MAD. JUST A LITTLE. I THOUGHT I MIGHT SIT ON YOUR DOORSTEP FOR THE NEXT FEW WEEKS. I'LL SCARE AWAY THOSE MONSTERS I CAN SEE FLYING OVER YOUR ROOF. WHAT? CAN'T YOU SEE THEM? ALL I WANT IS SOME FOOD? NO? THEN YOU COULD ALWAYS GIVE ME SOME *MONEY* TO GO AND BUY SOME. I'D HAVE TO GO AWAY THEN AND LEAVE YOU IN PEACE! PITY ABOUT THOSE FLYING MONSTERS. HELLO?

You may be given money to go away. Naturally, you won't *stay* away! If someone is daft enough to pay you then go back to them. They will probably be daft enough to pay you *again* ... and again!

If that doesn't work try being...

## A jarckman - an approved beggar

GOOD AFTERNOON, SIRS AND MADAMS. I AM AN OFFICIAL BEGGAR. I HAVE A LICENCE TO BEG, AS YOU CAN SEE. IT'S NOT THAT I AM TOO LAZY TO WORK. THIS LICENCE CONFIRMS THAT I AM IN FACT TOO SICK TO WORK. WOULD YOU CARE TO READ IT? YOU WILL SEE THAT THE MAGISTRATE WHO SIGNED IT IS FROM A TOWN A HUNDRED MILES FROM HERE BUT I CAN ASSURE YOU THAT IT IS OFFICIAL. PEOPLE LIKE YOU, WITH MONEY, REALLY OUGHT TO GIVE TO *OFFICIAL* BEGGARS LIKE ME

A licence to beg is very hard to get. However, if you know someone who can write, then you can make a forged licence, can't you? Just make sure that the local constable can't check up on the magistrate who was supposed to have signed it.

What if you're female? No problem. Become…

## A bawdy basket

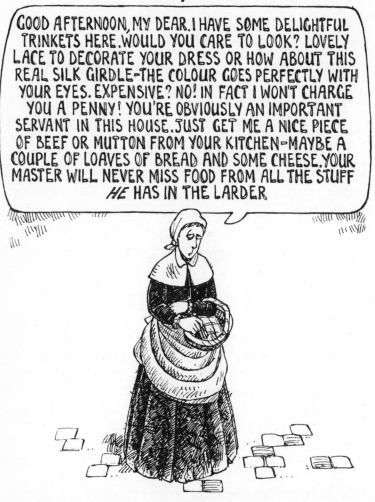

GOOD AFTERNOON, MY DEAR. I HAVE SOME DELIGHTFUL TRINKETS HERE. WOULD YOU CARE TO LOOK? LOVELY LACE TO DECORATE YOUR DRESS OR HOW ABOUT THIS REAL SILK GIRDLE - THE COLOUR GOES PERFECTLY WITH YOUR EYES. EXPENSIVE? NO! IN FACT I WON'T CHARGE YOU A PENNY! YOU'RE OBVIOUSLY AN IMPORTANT SERVANT IN THIS HOUSE. JUST GET ME A NICE PIECE OF BEEF OR MUTTON FROM YOUR KITCHEN - MAYBE A COUPLE OF LOAVES OF BREAD AND SOME CHEESE. YOUR MASTER WILL NEVER MISS FOOD FROM ALL THE STUFF *HE* HAS IN THE LARDER

Just make sure the lace and silk are as cheap as you can get them – and make sure the servants get you food or drink that is worth ten times as much!

If it all fails then try good old-fashioned lying as…

## A frater

GOOD MORNING, MADAM. IT'S A LOVELY DAY, ISN'T IT? THE SORT OF DAY WHEN YOU ARE GLAD TO BE ALIVE AND WELL. OF COURSE, IT'S A PITY NOT EVERYONE CAN BE WELL. THERE ARE SOME VERY SICK PEOPLE IN THIS TOWN. THE COUNCIL HAVE APPOINTED ME TO COLLECT FROM KIND AND GENEROUS CITIZENS LIKE YOURSELF. WE ARE PLANNING TO BUILD A HOSPITAL FOR THE SICK AND THE AGED. IF YOU COULD SPARE A FEW GROATS THEN YOU CAN BE SURE IT WILL GO TO A REALLY GOOD CAUSE

The truth is that *you* are that 'really good cause' and all money collected will go straight into your pocket.

These tricks may seem silly to you. You may say you would never be caught out by people like this. But the truth is millions of people *were* tricked into giving money to fraters and jarckmen and all their crooked kind. And, amazingly, they still are today.

In June 1995 a man and his wife were sentenced to jail for collecting thousands of pounds for a 'charity' that never existed.

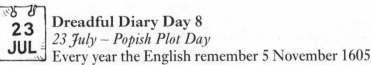

**Dreadful Diary Day 8**
*23 July – Popish Plot Day*
Every year the English remember 5 November 1605 when Guy Fawkes and his Catholic friends planned to blow up King James.

But the English *forget* the 'Popish Plot' of 1678 ... the plot that never was.

A man called Titus Oates dreamed up a story about a Catholic plot to murder Charles II. A French army would invade, Titus said. They would replace Charles II with his Catholic brother, James.

Oates was a greedy, dishonest (and smelly) man who hoped to make some money out of his lies. The English people believed terrible Titus and panicked.

People in Dorset fled from the coast in terror. They screamed...

But next morning, when the sun rose...

In London the council put great chains across the main streets to stop a French army charging down on their horses.

Dressmakers cashed in by selling knife-proof silk dresses.

And, of course, the English started attacking innocent Catholics. Many were tortured and about 35 Catholics were executed.

For nothing.

No plot. No invasion. No danger.

On 23 July 1679 two innocent Catholics, Philip Evans and John Lloyd, were sentenced to die. A notice was sent to the jail to give them the bad news. Unlike the folk of Dorset, Evans did NOT panic. He said to the messenger...

CAN'T READ IT NOW OLD CHAP. I WANT TO FINISH MY GAME OF TENNIS FIRST

While he waited to be hanged he calmly played the harp in his cell. Cool or what?

At last Oates was shown to be a liar – too late to save people like Evans and Lloyd. He was dragged through the streets of London and whipped.

**23 JUL** **Celebrate this day:**
Have a bonfire and burn a dummy of Titus Oates. Raise money for fireworks by begging – but don't cry 'A penny for the Guy!' Double your money by asking, 'Twopence for the Titus! Or 'An orful lot for the Oates!' OR have a game of tennis.

# Gorgeous Georgians and vile Victorians

Along came machines.

Around the 1780s the 'Industrial Revolution' started to grow in England. Suddenly people didn't have to work so hard. The Industrial Revolution meant one machine did the work of ten sweating men and women. Oh boy, oh joy! Were the English people happy?

There's no pleasing some people, is there?

The poor went to work on the machines even though they were very dangerous. In Wolverhampton a boy lost all his fingers in a nail-making machine – he was nine years old. Shame, he'd never get to count to ten.

But machines could make things faster and cheaper than humans. So the bosses could make lots of lovely loot while the workers were little better than slaves. (They staggered home to filthy slum houses where they could look forward to an early death from some dreadful disease.)

And machines made a huge difference to the wars the English fought. No more chopping and hacking at an enemy till you both got tired and went home.

112

Of course the machines won in the end. They always do.

## Terrible timeline

**1714** Now a German family takes the English throne. They are still there today. George I from Hanover becomes King of England and, like William the Conqueror almost 650 years before, doesn't even speak the English language.

**1745** The Scots are revolting. They want the old Stuarts back on the throne. Bonnie Prince Charlie leads their rebellion – he's not very bonnie but he looks a complete Charlie when his tartan army is crushed at the Battle of Culloden. The last great battle on British soil.

**1753** Here's a good way to make money – charge people to drive along the roads. (London remembered this in 2003 with its 'Congestion Charge'. But it's an old idea.) Many people hated paying money at the gates – the 'Turnpikes' as they were called. In West Yorkshire they tore them down. What did the government do? Sent the army to 'control' them. At least ten protesters are killed. That's controlled them then.

**1780** Gordon Riots. Now an English *lord* is leading riots (against the Catholics this time). Lord George Gordon heads the riots that go on for a week. Five hundred people are hurt. The mob tear holes in a prison roof, and captives escape. People shut themselves up in the London streets. The escaping prisoners rattle their chains at them. Creepy.

**1802** In Cornwall, Richard Trevithick invents a high-pressure steam engine so it can be used to drive a vehicle. Within a 100 years it'll be goodbye to horse-power and hello to trains and cars. Hedgehogs will pay the price.

**1805** Britain is in the middle of yet another war against France. Hero sailor Admiral Lord Nelson cops a French bullet at the Battle of Trafalgar. At least he gets a nice statue on a column in a London square – Trafalgar Square. Nelson was pickled in a barrel of brandy to keep him fresh for the journey home.

**1811** The poor workers blame the machines for their low wages and long hours. So they wreck the machines, and are known as 'Luddites' because their leader is supposed to be a man called General Ned Ludd – though he may never have existed.

**1834** Slavery is banned by Britain but women and little children will still work like slaves in England's mines until 1842 and the filthy factories for much longer. Instead of rioting the workers form a 'Trades Union' so they can go on strike. When men in Tolpuddle (Dorset) try this great idea they are sentenced to seven years in Australian prisons. (They are told to hop it to the land of the kangaroos.)

**1838** The 'Chartists' want every man to have a vote and think that will make their lives better. But the government ignores them so it's back to the old riots again. Notice they don't want women to have the vote. The cheek of it.

### English heroes

Newspapers are always going on about English heroes and how English children don't know enough about them.

The one 'hero' they always mention is...

**Lord Horatio Nelson (1758–1805) – admiral**
Nelson is a good English hero who spouted jolly good 'English' ideas. He once told a young sailor...

*First. Obey orders without thinking or asking questions.[1]*
*Second. Anyone who speaks badly about the king is your enemy.*
*Third. Hate all Frenchmen as you would the devil.*

Then Nelson probably went off to throw up because he suffered from seasickness.

His most famous saying was 'England expects every man to do his duty.' He did. He lost an eye and an arm in land battles but he still wasn't satisfied that he'd done enough 'duty' for England.

He did a very English thing by going off and getting himself shot on duty – while fighting the French at the Battle of Trafalgar. He once wrote, *'My blood boils at the name of a Frenchman.'*

Maybe he should have said…

MY BLOOD SPILLS AT THE NAME OF A FRENCHMAN

1 You can see why some teachers want you to treat Nelson as a hero.

Nelson died very prettily, which always helps if you want to be a hero. Of course Nelson's secretary, John Scott, also died in that battle. But he died *messily*. He was sliced in half by a cannon-ball and the two bits were thrown over the side to stop the sailors slipping on the slime.

There is a lesson there, young English readers.

*Hero*

DIE GRACEFULLY IN THE ARMS OF YOUR FRIENDS MUTTERING SOME 'FAMOUS LAST WORDS'

KISS ME, HARDY

*Not Hero*

DIE MESSILY SPLATTERED ALL OVER YOUR FRIENDS WITH ONE UN-FAMOUS LAST WORD

OUCH!

**Horrible history heroes**

Americans like to shoot at their presidents. And Americans love the presidents who are shot. President Lincoln and President Kennedy were shot dead and became huge heroes.

Shooting the prime minister is not a very English hobby. Maybe that's why the only English prime minister to be assassinated is *forgotten*. He SHOULD be a hero – dying on duty like that.

If you don't fancy Nelson as a hero then try...

**117**

### Spencer Perceval (1762–1812) – prime minister

Spencer Perceval was prime minister in 1812. His many enemies called him 'Little P'. He tried to deal with the 'Luddite' machine-wreckers by being really cruel to the ones who were caught. But it wasn't the Luddites who got him. It was an angry man called Henry Bellingham who blamed Perceval for losing his money in a bad deal. Bellingham walked into Parliament and shot Perceval.

Bellingham was just a rotten businessman – but a very good shot. Bellingham was arrested, tried and hanged within a week of shooting. Mrs Little P was given £50,000 (worth about £2 million today) so she'd be pleased. But not as pleased as the Luddites.

In the Midlands they ran through the streets, shouting...

Want to be a *Horrible Histories* hero? Then do what Little P did and make a lot of people very happy ... even if it means getting yourself shot.

### Captain James Cook (1728–1779) – explorer

Maybe the English should have a peaceful hero – not a fighter like Nelson. Someone like the great explorer, Captain Cook.

The English are famous for loving their dogs. But that doesn't stop them being extremely cruel to the miserable mutts.

Captain Cook was the first English person to sail to Australia. But his ships also came across a lot of Pacific Islands where the crew were very good at making enemies.

When some of Cook's men went ashore in New Zealand to get fresh water they vanished. More men went after them and saw the Maori natives having a feast. There were baskets in front of them and inside the baskets were the heads of the missing sailors.

You can guess what the Maoris were eating.

The sailors rushed back to their ship and begged Captain Cook to organize a revenge attack. He refused. So the sailors took their own very nasty piece of revenge.

The next time they landed they captured a Maori *dog*. They then...

- accused the dog of being a cannibal
- put it on trial
- found it guilty
- hanged it for its 'crime'
- ate it

A dog died horribly so that Captain Cook could be given a message from his men...

Maybe Captain Cook should have listened to them. In 1779 he landed in Hawaii and was killed and eaten by cannibals.

It seems his men didn't do a lot to stop them.

Want to be a hero?

Get yourself eaten and cooked ... like Cook!

## Peek at the pitiful

Want a laugh today in England? Then switch on the television. But what did the English do for fun before television was invented in the twentieth century? They went to visit and gawp at mentally ill people in the London lunatic asylum known as 'Bedlam'.

In the 1770s it was the biggest show in England. 1,00,000 people each year paid a penny each to see the human zoo. Mentally ill men women and children behaving wildly in their cells.

What could you see for your penny?
- A half-naked woman chained to a wall, howling like a wolf. Her legs were covered in rat-bites from her little 'friends' in the cell.
- Patients forced to drink poisonous mercury mixtures to shock them out of their illness.
- Nurses flogging the patients as 'treatment' – but they also did it for sport.
- Doctors slicing open veins in patients' arms and legs to let out blood and 'cool down' the brain fever.
- Screaming patients fastened to a wall with an iron hoop round the neck. They had buckets of icy water thrown over them.

And that was the GOOD news! All those visitors could see what was going on. When visiting was cut then the nurses could get away with more dreadful cruelties.

Nurses would use torture machines like a rack or pull out fingernails and toenails to punish their patients.

THIS MAY HURT A TEENSY BIT

They could brand patients with hot irons or use a roller on their backs that was studded with spikes. Some problem patients would be tied up, locked in a dark cell and starved till they were too weak to make any more trouble.

*Did you know...?*
The Bedlam hospital was first opened in 1247 by nuns for the sick. In 1370 it took in its first 'lunatics'. They were called that because they thought the madness was caused by the moon – that 'lunar' lump in the sky.

The nuns' first cures were usually forms of 'exorcism' – driving out the devils that caused the madness.

By 1815 Bedlam was closed.

## Manic music hall

English people in the 1800s and early 1900s enjoyed a bit of fun while they had a few drinks. So many pubs had stages and put on shows for their customers. They became known as 'music halls' and some great comics and singers went on those stages.

Those crowded bars could also be dangerous. A fight broke out in the Liverpool Colosseum in 1871. Someone shouted 'Fire!' ... which was a bit of a daft thing to do. 4,000 people panicked and rushed to the doors.

They piled into the corridors and stairways, tumbling and crushing people beneath them.

Rescuers arrived outside and started to PULL the people jammed in the doorways.

What went wrong?

**a)** They pulled the wall down and BLOCKED the doorway, making it worse.

**b)** They fastened ropes to horses and to stuck people but the horses ran off and dragged them to their deaths.

**c)** The rescuers pulled so hard – and the victims were so stuck – they just pulled the arms and legs clean off.

*Answer:*
c) Yeuch. Thirty-seven people died – or 36 and ten-tenths by the time they'd gathered all the bits together.

**27 AUG** **Dreadful Diary Day 9**
*24 August – St Bartholomew's Fair Day OR Dead Elephant Day*

On 24 August everybody used to go to the fair. It was St Bartholomew's Day and there were St Bartholomew's Fairs all over England.

St Bartholo ... *who?*

Bartholomew was a Christian saint who lived in Palestine. He died when his enemies skinned him alive.

Nice.

The biggest St Bart's Fair was in London and it happened every year from 1133 till 1855. Then it was banned by the killjoys because the crowds became too rough and violent – a bit like an England football match today.

Some of the most popular shows at the fair were 'Freak' shows where people went to gaze and poke at odd creatures. You could see...

Most amazing of all was 'The Invisible Girl'. No book has ever published a picture of this incredible sight. But here in this *Horrible Histories* book we have the very first picture of her EVER...

The greatest showman in England in the early 1800s was George Wombwell, who had a great story to tell...

I was born in Essex in 1777 and had a steady job as a cobbler in London. Then in 1800 a strange chance came my way. Two boa constrictor snakes were found in a ship in London docks.

I used every penny I had and bought them for £70. I started charging people to see them in the London taverns and I got my £70 back in three weeks. So I started buying more animals.

After ten years I set off to travel the
country with my show – Wombwell's
Travelling Menagerie, I called it. I went
to every cor er of the British
Isles in my brightly coloured
wagons.

They had jungle scenes on the outside and
wildcats, wolves, monkeys, giraffes, elephants
and camels on the inside. I became so
famous I gave three royal performances
before Queen Victoria herself.

Of course other people tried to copy me.
Villains like that Atkins. Every year we
met at the London Bartholomew's Fair.
One year I had such a struggle to get
there over the bad roads our old
elephant died.

It should have been a tragedy. Atkins gloated. He put up a sign over his show saying, 'See the only live elephant in the Fair.' So I put up a sign saying, 'See the only dead elephant in the Fair.' What happened?

Why, the crowds flocked to see my dead elephant – to prod it and poke it and gawp. As for Atkins' elephant? Hardly anyone went to see it at all! Oh, I did enjoy that!

Wombwell died in 1850 and *The Times* newspaper said…

No one has done so much as Wombwell to help the study of natural history among the common people. He bred the first African lion to be born in Britain. He called it 'Wallace' after the Scottish hero.

But that doesn't tell the *Horrible Histories* truth. Here is what they DON'T tell you…

As a publicity stunt, Wombwell advertised that he planned to set his lions against bull-mastiff dogs.

The idea was to let six dogs fight against Wombwell's pet lion, Nero. Unfortunately, for the bloodthirsty crowd, Nero refused to fight the dogs. The lion was well known for being tame.

So Wombwell put Wallace into the pit. Wallace gave such dreadful injuries to the dogs that the fight had to be abandoned.

Queen Victoria didn't get to see *that* sick show, you can bet.

**27 AUG** **Celebrate this day:**
Go to your nearest fair and eat a toffee apple. (They were first seen at Bartholomew's Fair as honey-coated apples.) OR go to your nearest fair and eat a dead elephant – ask for a jumbo burger.

# Woe for workers

In the Middle Ages the peasants were kept in their place by the bullying lords.

After the 1750s the workers were kept in their place by bullying bosses. Different leaders ... but the same suffering for the people who did the work.

PUT YOUR BACK INTO IT YOU LAZY, GOOD-FOR-NOTHING PLEB!

### Lynching Luddites
New machines put men out of work in the north of England. The working men ganged together to...
• smash the machines
• attack the bosses after dark
• capture new machines that were being carried to the factories
• fight battles against the army sent in to guard the bosses and the factories
• send threats to bosses saying, 'Get rid of the machines or we'll get rid of you.'
The men called themselves 'Luddites' – when they sent a threat they signed it General Ned Ludd. One very violent letter was sent from Chesterfield...

> Master William
>
> I am going to tell you that there is 6,000 men coming to get you in April. Then we will blow the houses of parliament up. Us working people can't stand it no more. The English governors are all rogues. We will soon have the great Revolution then all those great men's heads goes off.
>
> Signed
> General Ned Ludd

'General Ned Ludd' may have just been a name, though. There may have been no real man called that.

The English workers did the usual when they had a problem – rioted and sang a song...

*You can guard them with soldiers along the highway*
*Or closely locked up in a room.*
*Ned smashes them up, by night and by day,*
*And nothing can soften their doom.*

FACTORY

129

It was tough for the Luddites who were caught, though. Three were hanged and cut up at York Castle for shooting a mill owner near Huddersfield. All three men could prove that they were somewhere else when the man was killed.

It made no difference. They were butchered ... and nothing could soften *their* doom.

## Wotten weaving

When the machines came the bosses made them go as fast as possible to make as much money as possible. Now the workers had to keep up with the machines – or else.

Weaving cloth became hard and dangerous and there was no rest. If a machine threw a shuttle off, and it hurt you, then no one had time to stop and help.

Bosses fined you for being late and you only just made enough money to eat. What did the English do?

The usual: had a riot and wrecked machines ... and sang a song. One weaver's song, 'Poverty Knock', gives you a good idea of the tough work...

> *Up every morning at five,*
> *I wonder that we keep alive.*
> *Tired and yawning,*
> *Another cold morning,*
> *It's back to the dreary old drive.*

*Oh dear we're going to be late.*
*Gaffer is stood at the gate.*
*We're out of pockets,*
*Our wages they'll docket,*
*We'll have to buy grub on the slate.*

*Sometimes a shuttle flies out*
*and gives some poor woman a clout.*
*There she lies bleeding*
*But nobody's heeding,*
*Oh who's going to carry her out?*

The 'Gaffer' is the boss, of course. 'Docket' means 'cut'. Buying grub 'on the slate' meant paying for it later – if they ever made enough money.

*Did you know…?*
In 1830 children as young as seven worked from 6 a.m. till 7 p.m. in the dangerous cloth-weaving factories of Lancashire.

BUT WE DID GET 30 MINUTES FOR DINNER

In the potteries region (the English Midlands) tiny children could even start at 3 a.m. to work 16 or 18 hours a day.

The wage for one whole factory family in 1835 was about 50p a week.

**131**

### Pop goes the bottle girl's job

By the end of the 1800s, workers had won the right to go on strike. But it didn't do them a lot of good. Very often the bosses just brought in other people to do their job, so the workers starved and gave in.

Take the case of the Idris Soft Drinks Factory workers in 1910. The bosses wanted to cut the bottle-washers' pay of 45p a week.[1] So…

• The women formed a union to fight for their rights.
• The boss sacked the leader of the union.
• The women went on strike.
• The boss got boys to do their job.
• The penniless women had to go back to work.

What could they do? Sing a song!

In 1911 a popular song was sung to tell their story and to raise money. It was sung to the popular tune, 'All the nice girls love a sailor', and it shows that peasant workers STILL thought of the lords as the enemy. In one verse they sing…

*Oh you great king in the palace*
*And you statesman at the top,*
*When you're drinking soda water*
*Or supping ginger pop,*
*Think of some who work at Idris*
*For very little pay*
*And who only get nine bob[1]*
*For a most unpleasant job,*
*Alackaday, alackaday.*

They also sang a plea to the boys who stole their jobs…

1 That's 45p for a week's work washing bottles. You wouldn't even wash your parents' car for that, would you?

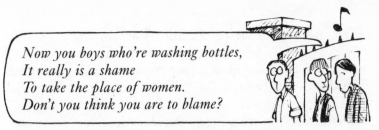

> *Now you boys who're washing bottles,*
> *It really is a shame*
> *To take the place of women.*
> *Don't you think you are to blame?*

But in four years' time those 'boys' would have more to worry about than washing bottles and more to fear than angry women.

In 1914 the frightful First World War started and the young men joined the army to march off and be slaughtered by German machine guns.

### Mining misery

In the early 1800s the most dangerous and dirty job of all was coal-mining. A mine inspector said...

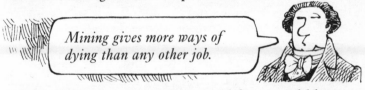

> *Mining gives more ways of*
> *dying than any other job.*

Men and women went underground for up to 16 hours a day. The more they dug out the more they were paid.

If a husband and wife were down the mine then what happened to the children? They couldn't afford to send them to school so they took them underground.

By the age of five the coal-covered kids were given a job as a 'trapper'. A trapper's job was to sit by the doors in the tunnels and open them every time a coal truck came along.

Easy? You could do that! Except...

- It was very dark and you had to listen for the trucks coming – if you failed to open the door it would smash and you'd be in trouble.
- You were paid a penny a day – but if you bought a candle then it cost a halfpenny a day ... so most trappers sat in the dark.

- You were out of bed at 4 a.m. to start work and worked all day. If you fell asleep it could be a disaster.
- There were no toilets down there. You did what you had to do in a corner of the tunnel – and so did everyone else. Poo!

Here are the top ten ways to die in a mine, just from one year, 1838 – which would you prefer?

Note: In 1873 James Morrow, aged eight, fell asleep while trapping. A coal truck sliced off his leg. James had a wooden leg fitted and went back down the mine a few months later. A roof collapsed and crushed him to death soon after. Not a lucky boy.

Note: Miners took canaries down the mine. If the canary fell off its perch it had been gassed. Time to get out before the gas got you next.

Note: On Wednesday, 8 September 1880, at Seaham (County Durham) more than 160 lives were lost in an explosion. Yet another 83 men died in another explosion at Seaham in 1951. You'd have thought things would get better.

Note: At Earsdon (Northumberland) in 1862 the lift machine collapsed and trapped 204 men and boys. That was the only way out. They all died. William Gledson was 71 years old. John Armstrong was just 10. He died alongside his father.

Note: In 1925 miners at the Montagu Pit in Newcastle dug through rock straight into an old flooded mine. Thirty-eight died. A map of the old mine would have helped them to avoid it. They didn't have a map: a piece of paper that would have saved 38 lives.

Other ways to die? How about these...

**The worst disaster**
In 1838 the Moorend Pit (North Yorkshire) started to fill with water when a thunderstorm struck. Hailstones the size of a fist damaged the steam engine that worked the lift. Streams burst their banks and began to rush down the mine shaft.

The miners escaped but the children were told to go to the 'Day Hole' for safety. It was the deepest part of the pit – the only part that filled to the top with icy water.

It flooded. Fifteen boys and 11 girls drowned.

The oldest was 17.

The youngest, Joseph Burkinshaw, was seven years old and died with his ten-year-old brother George.

Sarah Newton was eight.

A week after they were buried there was an explosion in a steam-engine at a nearby pit. A boy had his head blown off.

**Money-making mine-owners**
Just as in ancient England, the lords with the land made the money. John Micklethwaite owned the Oaks Colliery near Barnsley. He told a mines inspector…

*The mine is run by my manager. I only ride over here for amusement. I have never been in the pit and I never will. I don't know if we have boys and girls under the age of eight … ask my manager!*

Not only did the landlords sell the coal and make a profit. They paid the miners with one hand and took it back with the other.

Work for the master or die. Slavery did not disappear with the Middle Ages.

Six-year-old John Saville of Sheffield told an inspector…

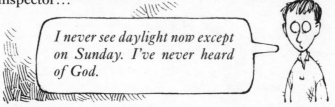

*I never see daylight now except on Sunday. I've never heard of God.*

Maybe God had forgotten John and his friends.

Mine-owners had heard of God, and went to church each Sunday – but that didn't change their ways.

'LAND OF HOPE AND GLORY, MOTHER OF THE FREE'

HOPE?  FREE?

# Kruel for kids

It hasn't always been easy being young in England. Here are a few horrible historical tales of tots and teens...

**1 Misery Mary**
Around the year 1700 Mary Channing was just 14 when her parents forced her to marry a boring and smelly old grocer, Richard Channing.

By the time she was 19 she'd had enough so she poisoned him. Naughty girl. But she didn't deserve her cruel punishment.

She was taken to the old stone circle known as Maumbury Rings near Dorchester. Over 10,000 people gathered to watch her being strangled. Then they cheered as her body was burned.

In 1767 people were still being taken to the ancient circle to be executed in public. But none was as young, or as sad, as Mary.

**2 Deadly dad**
In 1858 little Anna Burgess lived with her father, William, on Exmoor (Somerset). One day he killed her and buried her in a field.

But big, bad Burgess panicked. He was sure her body would be found, so he dug it up from the field. He then dropped it down an old mine shaft and burned her clothes.

Local people found the burned clothes but not the body.

Burgess would have got away with the kid-killing crime. Then local people saw a weird blue light flickering at the top of the mine shaft. Was it gas from the mine? Or was it the ghastly gassy spirit of Anna?

The people looked and found her little body.

Wicked William was hanged.

### 3 Foul for Fanny

In 1867 an eight-year-old girl called Fanny Adams was killed and chopped up in Alton, Hampshire. When the police caught up with Frederick Baker he had written in his diary...

24 August 1867
— Today I killed a girl —

Now that's nasty, but poor Fanny's death became a joke. Bits of her body were never found. At that time the Royal Navy were being fed cheap meat in tins. When they looked at the disgusting stuff they joked...

WHAT'S THIS THEN?

IT'S SWEET FANNY ADAMS

Now the phrase 'Sweet Fanny Adams' still means something worthless. Poor Fanny.

Baker was hanged ... on Christmas Eve.

HO, HO...

HO! cck

## 4 Nottingham nasties

Children make good hostages. After all, they don't cost as much to feed as adults and they aren't strong enough to fight their way to freedom.

Most of all their parents will behave themselves if you hold their kid prisoner and say...

DO AS YOU'RE TOLD OR THE KID GETS IT!

That's what King John did with his Welsh enemies. He took 28 boys as hostage. Of course King John wouldn't really hurt those little Welsh boys, would he?

Well, he did. He had all 28 taken to the top of Nottingham castle walls and thrown off with ropes around their necks.

## 5 Rotted rebel

When dad went to war the kids sometimes had to follow. An Irish weaver called Crosby joined the Jacobite rebellion of 1745–1746 and took his little son William along with him. The Scottish Jacobites were trying to put the Stuart Prince Charlie back on the English throne.

The Jacobites lost and were thrown into Carlisle prison to rot in the damp and stinking dungeons. The winners – who were happy with the German king from Hanover – decided to execute about 20 rebels and let the rebels choose who would go.

How would YOU decide which of your group of friends would go to have their heads cut off?

They drew straws. Here's how...

a. Cut five straws - four long and one short.

b. Hold the straws in one person's fist so the cut one is hidden.

c. Five people take turns to pick a straw.

d. The one who picks the short straw is the loser.

e. Carry on till 20 losers have been chosen.

f. Hack off the heads of the losers.[1]

The GOOD news? William wasn't executed.

The BAD news? He died of a fever in the slimy, stinking cell.

The VERY BAD news? William Crosby was just seven years old.

The executed Scots had their heads stuck on poles and the skulls were still there 30 years later.

## 6 Mill misery

At Colne Bridge in West Yorkshire there was a weaving mill. In 1818 the girls who worked there were 'trouble'. The owner decided to keep them under control. How?

He let them in to work, then bolted the doors. They couldn't get out till they had done their day's work. Sadly that was the day the mill caught fire. Seventeen girls died. The youngest were just nine years old.

1 Only joking. Hacking off heads is very dangerous. Do not try it. Find an adult to do it for you.

They didn't give any trouble after that – except to the gravedigger of Kirkheaton churchyard who had to dig 17 graves, of course.

## 7 Terrified Thomas

In the 1840s young Thomas Moorehouse was sent to work for a miner in North Yorkshire. It wasn't the work that bothered him. It was the way his cruel master treated him. Thomas said...

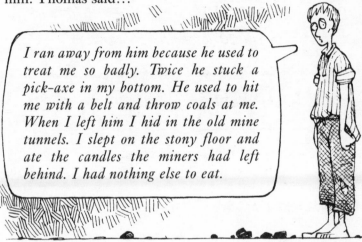

*I ran away from him because he used to treat me so badly. Twice he stuck a pick-axe in my bottom. He used to hit me with a belt and throw coals at me. When I left him I hid in the old mine tunnels. I slept on the stony floor and ate the candles the miners had left behind. I had nothing else to eat.*

And, of course, he would not be welcome back home. A doctor looked at him and found him covered in wounds from his master's belt.

Still, you learn a lot from horrible history. Now you know that, if you are ever starving, you can eat a candle ... and have a light snack.

## 8 Shocking school

English children did not see many horrors or war through the ages. Not like the children of Europe. But the 1900s brought air raids and bombs and death in the streets of England. One bomb dropped near the station at Cottingham (East Yorkshire) in 1915. A schoolgirl stepped off the train soon after and walked into a human slaughter-house. She said…

*The bomb had just destroyed the road I had to walk down to get to school. There were bodies and bits of bodies all over. There were heads, arms and legs blown into trees and everywhere and no one about. I walked into school, into the classroom and sat down. The first lesson was maths. I was in shock – not all there. I could hardly speak and even when I got home I didn't tell my parents what I'd seen. I wish I could have. The words just wouldn't come.*

It makes your trip to school look quite pleasant, doesn't it?

## Cruel schools

Cruel schools have been around for 1,000s of years. But in England in 1870…

And you still do. Of course school is not so easy now, but in the past public schools ran a sort of slave system where younger boys worked for the older boys and were bullied and beaten by them.

At Winchester School, for example, the older boys toughened up the young ones by making them hold burning sticks. At Rugby they were roasted over an open fire. At Eton in the 1700s a boy wrote home...

My Dearest Mama,
                          I wright to tell you I am very retched. I have not made any progress and I do not think I shall. I am very sorry to be an expense to you, but I do not think this schule is very good. One of the boys has been using my hat for target practice and there are black beetles in the food. I hope Matilda is better and I am glad she is not at schule. I think I have got consumption¹ and the boys at this place are not gentlemen but of course you did not know that when you sent me here. I will try not to get into bad habits. Don't mind my suffering because I don't think I shall last long please send me some money as I owe 8 pence
                          Your loving but retched son
                                                George

1 A deadly lung disease.

The biggest bully was head teacher Dr John Keat who whacked about ten boys every day with the cane – except Sundays when he had a day of rest. On 30 June 1832 he beat over 80 pupils on that one day.

What sort of jobs did the young boys have to do for the older ones? Making tea and cleaning boots were all right. But there were also odd things like...

And that's not ancient history. It still happened at Wellington School in 1959.

So now it's time to...

### Test your terrible teacher

History teachers love tests – they must do because they are always giving their lucky pupils brain-breaking questions. So, of course, they will just love it if you give them a simple test, won't they? They can show you how clever they really are. Just choose one of the three answers. Easy as ABC...

1 Everyone now knows you get the Black Death from flea bites. But there is another way of catching it that teachers never tell you. What?
a) scratching yourself on a rusty nail that a flea has landed on
b) eating food with fleas in
c) breathing in the germs on rat poo

**2** Archbishop Thomas à Becket was hacked to death in his cathedral. His bones were said to cure the sick. A boy was cured of a stomach worm.
How long was this worm?
**a)** 5 centimetres
**b)** 50 centimetres
**c)** 5 metres

**3** In the 1100s what was the punishment for forging money?
**a)** You had your hand and your naughty-bits chopped off.
**b)** You had your head cut off.
**c)** You had your fake coins melted down and the red-hot metal poured down your throat.

**4** In the 1200s the cure for toothache was what?
**a)** chip out the black bits with a hammer, then fill the hole with cement
**b)** burn the black bits with a candle
**c)** fill a hole in a tooth with crushed toenails and bees-wax

**5** Henry VIII said his new 'Church of England' would not have 'idols' – statues – like the Catholic churches had. So his men wrecked these idols. What else in England did they think about wrecking?
**a)** the Tower of London – because it was built by William the Conqueror who was a Catholic.
**b)** stonehenge – because it was a heathen place of worship.
**c)** all the houses in Pope Street (even though they were named after the discoverer John Pope and not THE Pope, head of the Catholics).

**6** In the 1500s you could be knocked out by a 'Left Leg'. How?

**a)** Soldiers were taught to kick troublemakers with their left leg and the left boot always had a special iron toe-cap.

**b)** When a sheep was killed its right leg was eaten first. The left leg was hung above the door to dry and careless visitors could smack their heads against it.

**c)** 'Left Leg' was the name of a type of strong beer and too much would knock you out.

**7** In the 1600s English people refused to eat this food because they said it was poisonous. What was it?

**a)** tomato
**b)** shark
**c)** hedgehog

**8** In the 1600s and 1700s most English men wore wigs if they could afford them. Why?

**a)** because there was a disease going around that meant most men were bald by the age of 22

**b)** because the kings wore wigs and everyone wanted to copy them

**c)** because it meant they could shave their heads and keep the head-lice away

**9** In 1620 there were 19 witches put on trial at Pendle (Lancashire). One dotty old lady was called Alice. Alice what?

**a)** Nutter
**b)** Batty
**c)** Brainless

**10** In 1912 a train crash at Hebden Bridge, Yorkshire, killed four people. But five people from the train were buried. How did that happen?
**a)** One of the people killed was a twin.
**b)** The train had a coffin and a corpse on board before it crashed.
**c)** One of the people on the train was buried alive.

---

*Answers:*

**1 c)** Yes, if you breathe in the scent of rat poo then you can catch the disease that the rat had. It's a fact, but no one has ever explained WHY you would want to go round sniffing rat poo. Anyone who does that DESERVES to die horribly.

**2 b)** Almost everyone had worms in their guts, but a worm as long as 50 cm was rare.

**3 a)** It was your right hand that was chopped off – which wasn't so bad if you were left-handed.

**4 b)** A doctor would tell you...

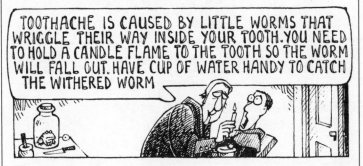

TOOTHACHE IS CAUSED BY LITTLE WORMS THAT WRIGGLE THEIR WAY INSIDE YOUR TOOTH. YOU NEED TO HOLD A CANDLE FLAME TO THE TOOTH SO THE WORM WILL FALL OUT. HAVE CUP OF WATER HANDY TO CATCH THE WITHERED WORM

I suppose if the flame didn't kill the worm it would drown in the water! And if you thought that toothache cure was bad, be glad it wasn't something else. The cure for some body pains was to hold red-hot irons against them.

**5 b)** It wasn't just statues that were smashed. Religious paintings on church walls were painted over. Some churches (like Stratford) painted over the pictures with thin paint that could be washed off later – they thought the Catholic religion might come back (and they were right!).

The paintings told stories from the Bible and were quite useful because most English people couldn't read – they learned the Bible stories from the pictures.

**6 c)** 'Left Leg' was served in the taverns where William Shakespeare lived and wrote and acted. Maybe the actors even had a cup of it before they went on stage.

**7 a)** And they could have been right! Posh people ate off plates made of pewter – a metal made with lead. Tomatoes on pewter could make a nasty poison mixture that made you ill.

The poor ate off wooden plates and didn't have that problem – but then the poor could not afford tomatoes.

**8 c)** This is extremely cruel to the lice, of course, who had no nice men's hair to crawl around in. Why couldn't the men offer these poor nits good homes? They could always scratch their heads if they got too tickly. And those horse-hair wigs the men wore were pretty hot and itchy anyway. A homeless louse had to stick to finding a woman. It's a lousy life.

**9 a)** Alice Nutter was hanged. Old Mother Demdike was accused of being a witch. To save herself she accused other old women in the area, including Alice Nutter. Many of the women she named were hanged at Lancaster jail. Mother Demdike was luckier – she died in her prison cell. Luckier? Well? Which way would you rather die?

**10 b)** The Liverpool to Leeds express went into the twisty stretch at Hebden Bridge too fast and jumped off the rails. Four people were killed when the front two coaches smashed. Many more were hurt – but not the man in the coffin ... at least he never complained.

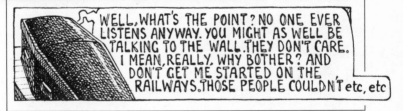

WELL, WHAT'S THE POINT? NO ONE EVER LISTENS ANYWAY. YOU MIGHT AS WELL BE TALKING TO THE WALL. THEY DON'T CARE. I MEAN, REALLY, WHY BOTHER? AND DON'T GET ME STARTED ON THE RAILWAYS. THOSE PEOPLE COULDN'T etc, etc

**6 DEC**

**Dreadful Diary Day 10**
*6 December – St Nicholas's Day OR Money-grabbing Day*

Christmas only happens once a year. Some greedy people would like it TWICE a year. Well, here is their chance. After all 6 December is St Nicholas's Day ... and St Nicholas, of course, is Santa Claus, the saint of children.

Why is Saint Nick the saint of children? Here's the story English children were told at Christmas. Our

Horrible Historians have uncovered a letter from a young man who wrote a letter home at the time. Here it is, this 1,700-year-old letter, published in a book for the first time. A *Horrible Histories* first and exclusive scoop...[1]

Myra
Turkey
AD 322

Dear Mum
   As you know I've got this great job here in Myra. I am second assistant to the deputy jailer. I get to keep the keys and feed the prisoners in the dungeons. I know you are worried because six boys like me have gone missing in the past month. But the man who has been disappearing them has been caught.
   Not only that but we have him right here in one of my cells now. His story is so disgusting I hope you are not eating dinner when you read this!

1 All right. We made the letter up, if you want to be picky. But read it anyway to get the story of St Nick. And if you want to be picky then pick your nose instead.

The villain is Michael the Taverner who owns the inn on the town square. Every night after work I used to go down there and eat some of his tasty pork stew. The Taverner is an evil-looking bloke. Hairy face, hairy hands and hairy arms. Here, I'll draw a picture to show you.

One day, after the Taverner had served me a lovely plate of stew, I decided I wanted some more, so I went through to the kitchen. He was taking some more pickled meat out of a barrel full of salt water. He slapped it on the table and was going to slice it up when he turned and saw me. 'Here!' I cried. 'That's a funny-looking pig's trotter!'

And it was. It looked more like a human leg to me. I've never seen a pig's foot with five toes before now. The Taverner just grabbed his knife and came after me.

He muttered something like, 'You're next sonny.'

I ran. Here I am running. I ran through the street till I got to the city guards. I told them what I'd seen. They didn't believe me at first. 'That Michael makes nice pork stew,' they said.

In the end they went back and searched the tavern kitchen. What do you think they found in the barrel of salt water? The chopped-up bits of three of the missing boys.

Some of the guards were sick in the street. I can't blame them. They called in Bishop Nicholas to give the boys a good funeral and he did an amazing thing. He laid out the pickled boy bits on the ground, covered with a cloth, then he said a few prayers and things. When he pulled back the cloth the boys were all joined together

again. Not only that but they were alive.
It was a miracle. They reckon Bishop
Nicholas should be made Saint Nicholas.
Here's what they looked like —

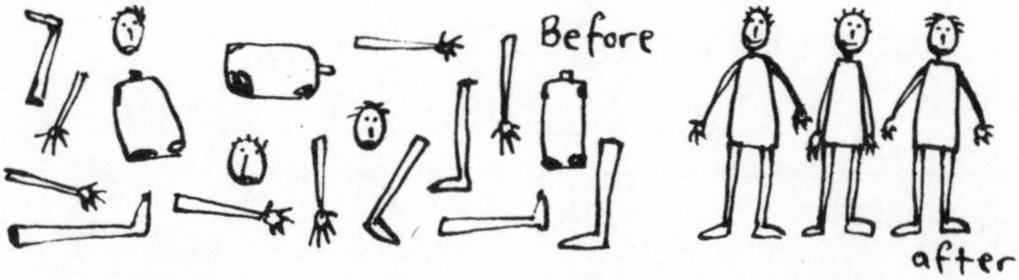

Before

after

Even though they were alive they still
charged the Taverner with murder and we'll
all go to watch him hang tomorrow. I took
him his bread today and I asked him,
'So what happened to the other three
missing boys?'
He just said, 'What do you think, you
simple boy?'
So I guess we'll never know.
But I will miss his tasty pork stew.

Your loving son,
Christopher
Second assistant to deputy jailer

On 6 December in England schoolboys used to have a day off to celebrate. A writer, John Aubrey, said...

> The schoolboys in the west of England were given a barrel of good ale on St Nicholas's day. That night they had the right to break down their teacher's cellar door.

Miserable old Henry VIII tried to put a stop to this. But he couldn't stop it everywhere in England. On this day some Tudor schoolboys...
- dressed up as priests, bishops and women
- went from house to house to 'bless' the people inside – and be paid money
- went to church and acted as preachers for the day.

**6 DEC** **Celebrate this day:** Eat some tasty pork stew OR dress up as a priest and go from door to door, blessing people ... in exchange for some cash.

# Terrible 20th century

Just when you thought it was the 'modern' age and it was safe to live in England along came some new horrors to shock, sicken, disgust and kill you. That's life.

### Terrible timeline

**1905** Women decide they want the vote. So they starve themselves with hunger strikes, set fire to buildings and make a real nuisance of themselves till they get what they want.

**1914** The First World War starts against Germany (and goes on till 1918). The posh young men are the officers and they lead the poor young men who are the soldiers into German machine guns. England wins. Germany loses. The men who make the war machines and ships and guns and planes win most of all. The rioting English wreck German bakers' shops in London.

**1918** War ends and women win the vote. Were they grateful? Mrs Pankhurst said the War had been God's revenge on the men who had refused to give women the vote. If that were true then God must be pretty cruel, mustn't she?

**1926** The 'General Strike'. Times are hard and the War has left many people worse off than they were before. Was it worth fighting and

dying for? No, so lots of workers gang together for a strike. The soldiers who were fighting for their country eight years ago are now fighting for themselves. Nothing new there then. Only the coal-miners stay out and suffer on strike. They are defeated by the villainous and hated minister, Winston Churchill.

**1939** Another war against Germany. By March 1940 Britain is led by the heroic and loved Winston Churchill. (Yes, the same man they hated in 1926.) This time those clever German flying machines will let you die for your country without having to leave the comfort of your own slum houses. Many English cities suffer – but then, so do many German cities. God's revenge again?

**1978** Those strikers are back. This is known as 'The Winter of Discontent'. Bin-men won't collect your rubbish so it piles up in the street. But most gruesome of all, gravediggers won't bury your dead. Where do you pile up the corpses?

**1984** This time it's the miners' turn to go on strike. No Winston Churchill to crush them this time, but they have Prime Minister Margaret Thatcher instead. After bitter battles with police the miners lose and have to go back to work or starve. The mines begin to close and soon there are not enough miners left to bother anyone.

**1989** The Poll Tax is back! It started the Peasants' Revolt back in 1381 and now the peasants revolt again. This time Prime Minister Thatcher is the loser. She loses her job. England loses the Poll Tax. Maybe there is hope for the peasants after all.

## Horrible Home Front

The First World War started on 4 August 1914 for Britain. Soon soldiers were marching along the streets of England, telling young men to join the army. They sang...

Awful song, but it seemed to work. A million men joined up to fight. A lot of them died.

A million workers flocked to the fight. Bullets and bombs were better than miserable mines and foul factories.

Most people have heard of the horrors of the war in Europe.[1] No one tells you of the horrible history of England during the war. Time to change that with a few foul facts about the home front...

1 See *Horrible Histories – Frightful First World War* for the soldiers' stories.

## Free feathers and blood

If a man refused to join the army he was called a coward. Women would torment him. They would hand him a white feather – a sign of a coward. They would also throw things into his garden.

## Ships and shells

The War came to England with a bang on the morning of 16 December 1914. German battleships arrived off the coast of Hartlepool in north-east England and turned their guns on the town. They killed nine soldiers – they also killed 97 men and women who were not fighters. Saddest of all they killed 37 children. One was just six months old.

A boy described a small miracle...

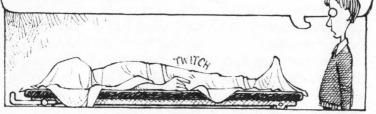

*They told us my sister was dead. We went to have one last look at her as she lay dead in the hospital. She was covered in a white sheet. As I looked I saw the sheet move. Her finger gave a small twitch. She was alive! The doctors took her away and cured her. She was just an hour away from being nailed in her coffin.*

The girl lived a long life after that.

### Foul for foreigners
English people learned to hate Germans living in England and started attacking them. They said...
• German waiters would poison your soup
• German watchmakers were making time-bombs
• and as for a German barber, he would cut your throat
Lies, of course, but German shopkeepers in England had their windows broken and their goods stolen.

### Nasty for nurses
When the fighting started there were huge numbers of wounded men. The ones who lived were sent back to England. Suddenly England was full of sick and injured soldiers. There weren't enough nurses to care for so many of them.

So ordinary women gave their help to the hospitals. At least, they tried, but some were not very good.

One young nurse had never seen a man with his clothes off before, but she was ordered to wash a naked man. His skin looked very dark so she scrubbed and scrubbed. It didn't work! Then another nurse told her...

### Zapped by Zeppelins
The Germans began to send bombers over England in 1915. They were not aeroplanes but huge airships called Zeppelins.

The crew of a Zeppelin would pick up a bomb and drop it over the side of the cabin. They were rotten shots – even if they were aiming to wreck English stations or factories they usually missed and killed ordinary people in their homes instead.

That's why Zeppelins got a new nickname…

These attacks were not as bad as the 'Blitz' of the Second World War, 25 years later. There were just over 50 Zeppelin raids in 45 months and never more than a dozen Zeppelins at a time. But they forced the English to turn out all the lights so the Zeppelins couldn't find the towns. These 'blackouts' caused more trouble than the Zeppelins themselves.

One boy ran for home when a Zeppelin was spotted – but in the blackout he ran into a lamp-post and knocked himself out.

### Horrible hunger

Food became hard to find as the War went on. Many families went hungry. What could they do about it? A group of children in Usworth, County Durham, went on strike.

They said...

In London a woman walked into a butcher shop and spotted a piece of meat...

1917 was a year of hunger when...
- Some children had to eat dandelion-leaf sandwiches.
- A boy from Lavenham (Suffolk) helped his dad poach rabbits. He said he liked eating the rabbit head for dinner, sucking out the tasty brains.
- Farmers threw turnips into the fields for sheep to eat. Children pinched them from the sheep and ate them raw.

## Simply striking

The longer the War went on the more fed up the English became. Men in the coal-mines and steelworks knew they were important. They went on strike for more money.

The government paid them rather than lose the precious coal – but they would get their own back (and get their money back) in the 1920s when the War ended.

Steelworkers in Sheffield sang a song to the Prime Minister, Lloyd George, telling him they were too good to go off and fight in France...

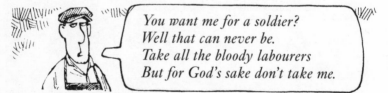

*You want me for a soldier?*
*Well that can never be.*
*Take all the bloody labourers*
*But for God's sake don't take me.*

The English workers made trouble, but they never had a revolution. In Russia the workers took over the country and the royal family were massacred.

## World War working women

Women were never treated as well as men. In the early twentieth century, they were not allowed to vote or become a Member of Parliament. When the First World War took the men off to fight, the women took their jobs and got a lot of respect. At the end of the War they got the vote they'd fought for for so long. But that war work could sometimes be as dangerous as the fighting.

Women often worked with explosives to make bullets and bombs. One spark could kill dozens in the factory. In July 1918 an explosion at Chilwell (Nottingham) killed 134 people. Most of them were women. A boy was playing in the area and described the horrible sight.

*A wagon came past me and I could smell burning rags. It was stacked with bodies, maybe twenty of them, tied down with ropes. Half their clothes had been scorched off and arms and legs hung over the side. There was a trail of blood behind the wagon.*

Not all the horrors were in the French trenches.

### Pain of the Pals

Millions of ordinary men joined the army to fight in France. Many had the bright idea of joining all together in the same regiment of the army. They called themselves 'Pals' – the Sheffield Pals or the Burnley Pals. The trouble was that when a regiment was smashed by the German machine guns those Pals died together. Towns and villages lost dozens of young men at the same time.

And families too. A woman in King's Lynn (Norfolk) lost all three of her sons in one battle. A London woman lost her husband and son to the same German shell.

In England the news was carried back to the families by little post boys. Families got to dread those little boys tapping at the door.

**Vain victory**

The soldiers were told they'd return to a better England; to a 'land fit for heroes'. Of course it never happened. It never does. Still, they did return to a changed place.

The English had fought side by side with Scots, Irish and Welsh, not to mention others from the British Empire. They even fought alongside the oldest enemy of all, the French.

After four years of fierce fighting the English were changed. The War had made them British. They had fought side by side with their old masters – the upper classes. England and the English would never be the same again.

By 1945 a Second World War had seen bombs rained down on British cities and Mr Hitler's nasty Nazis defeated. People felt even more proud to be 'British'. For 50 years being 'English' didn't seem to matter much any more.

Then the Scots and Welsh decided they wanted a bit more freedom – their own parliaments – and that set the English thinking: 'Hey, if they've got their own parliaments why can't we have ours?'

See? It was that old enemy, the Scots again. That's why England should maybe have a holiday to celebrate beating the tartan terrors...

**Dreadful Diary Day 11**

9 **SEP**

*9 September – Flodden Day OR Killed Kilt Day*
The English have fought against just about everyone in the world at some time. But their oldest enemies are their nearest neighbours – the Scots.

On 9 September 1513 the English beat the Scots in the bloody Battle of Flodden Field in Northumberland.

Now usually you could feel sorry for the Scots when they lost – after all there are ten times as many English as there are Scots. But at Flodden they were asking for it.

HENRY VIII TOOK AN ENGLISH ARMY ACROSS THE CHANNEL TO FIGHT IN FRANCE

WHILE HE WAS AWAY THE FRENCH SENT AN ARMY UP TO SCOTLAND

THE FRENCH AND THE SCOTS INVADED ENGLAND FROM THE NORTH

SNEAKY!

SCOTLAND

ENGLAND

FRANCE

Henry had left his wife Catherine of Aragon in charge. The only real warrior left in England was the Earl of Surrey ... and he was 80 years old.

Old Surrey, in a hurry, was curried ... sorry, *carried* ... north and the armies met at Flodden Field.

There were 20,000 English against 30,000 Scots. Bad enough. But the Scots had some new pikes the French had given them. The Scots' pikes were 4.5 metres long and like a spear. The English pikes were just 2.5 metres tall and shaped like a hook.

**169**

You might imagine what would happen...

Well you'd be wrong! The English soldiers simply swiped the long, clumsy Scottish spears in half.

Scottish King James IV was killed in the battle and Queen Catherine sent his bloody coat over to Henry VIII in France as a charming gift.

How did Henry feel about this?

**a)** He was so thrilled he sent a chest of French silver back to Catherine.

**b)** He was so thrilled he sent a dead Frenchman's coat back to Catherine.

**c)** He wasn't thrilled at all. In fact he was furious.

*Answer:*
c) Henry was not doing very well in his French war.
When he learned his WIFE had done better than him
he was jealous and very angry.

**9 SEP**

**Celebrate this day:**
Get a bucket of blood from the butcher, dip an old coat in it and send the coat to the Queen. OR take a 2.5 metre pike, go to Flodden and see if you can find a wild haggis. If you do, then kill it.

# What's English?

It's no use asking an English person 'What makes an English person so English?' To get an honest picture you need to ask an enemy or two.

The foul French, for example, have fought wars WITH the English and AGAINST the English – the Hundred Years War between the two went on for 116 years. (That was all about the English kings who thought they should rule France.)

Of course, ever since William the Conqueror landed the French thought they should rule the English.

In the early 1200s a French bishop wrote what he thought about the English way of life...

*England is forever covered in ice and snow. The food is foul. The air is bad. The sea is full of monsters. The soil is not very rich. The people are heathens. The English language is fit for barbarians. But worst of all, they don't drink wine – they drink a dreadful stuff called beer that rots the belly.*

So there you have it. England is an awful place. But is the French bishop right about foul food, dreadful drink and 'barbarian' language?

172

## English is ... foul food

What's wrong with English food? Anyway, what IS English food?

### Beautiful beef
Roast beef was so popular in the Middle Ages it became the nickname for the English. The French called the English enemies 'rosbifs' – probably because they couldn't spell 'roast beefs'.

The truth is it was the *rich* English who ate the most roast beef. In 1542 a monk called Andrew Borde said...

*Beef is a Lord's dish and it makes an Englishman what he is – strong and healthy. Bacon is best for farmers and the poor eat porridge.*

WHAT HE SPRAYS IS TRUE

In 2003 France had another row with Britain about a war in Iraq and the French sprayed 'rosbifs get out' over some English war graves. After 700 years they still haven't learned how to spell.

### Filthy food
But Andrew Borde was right about poor people eating little but porridge.

In the Middle Ages, the poor cooked in the kitchen with a big pot (cauldron) that always hung over the fire. Every day they lit the fire and added things to the pot. They ate mostly peas to make pease porridge, and didn't get much meat.

173

They would eat the porridge for dinner, leaving left-overs in the pot to get cold overnight and then start over the next day. That stew must have had bits in it that had been there for quite a while. They even made that into a rhyme...

SNIFF

*Pease porridge hot,*
*Pease porridge cold,*
*Pease porridge in the pot,*
*Nine days old.*

*Did you know...?*
In times of famine the English ate worse than old porridge. One monkish writer in the Middle Ages, who wrote the *Annals of Bermondsey*, reckoned...

*Famine is so common that starving people are driven to eat dogs, cats, the droppings of doves and their own children.*

WOULDN'T YOU RATHER HAVE THIS YUMMY PIGEON POO?

## Fish and chips

Fried fish was sold in England in the 1800s – cooked in kitchens and taken round the streets to be sold with roast potatoes. Then, in 1865, the English borrowed an idea from the French – fried potatoes or chips. Fish and chips were born and the English loved them.

By the twentieth century there were 15,000 English fish and chip shops. (Only 8,500 now as burger bars take over.)

## English is ... dreadful drink

The English certainly like to drink – whether it's beer, wine and spirits, or just 'a nice cup of tea'...

### Bad booze

The night before the Battle of Hastings the Norman soldiers said their prayers while the English soldiers got drunk!

In fact, the English have around 2,000 words for getting drunk – from A to Z. (From 'A bit lit' to 'Zozzled', in fact.)

Here are ten English words. Nine of them can be used to describe someone who's drunk. Which is the odd one out?

You can say, 'This person is...'

> Odd one out: the third word, Trolleybags. That means a dirty and disgusting person – the sort of person who picks her nose before sticking her hand into your bag of crisps.

In 1742 about 5 million English people were drinking 20 million gallons of gin every year.

In the 1870s a Russian visitor was shocked by what he saw in an English pub...

*Everyone is drunk, but unhappy and gloomy and strangely silent. Only swearing and the odd bloody fight breaks the silence. Everyone is in a hurry to drink till they are senseless. The wives drink as much as the husbands and they all get drunk together while children crawl and run about among them.*

## Tea

In 1660 Samuel Pepys said...

*Today I drank a cup of tea – something I have never drunk before.*

As it cost £12 a kilo at the time – a fortune today – it's not surprising it took a while to catch on.

People think of tea as a very 'English' drink. But it wasn't until later in the 1600s when Queen Catherine arrived from Portugal (where tea was more common) and got the posh English people drinking it.

The poor copied the posh as soon as they could afford it. But they were often sold 'British Tea'. A little real tea mixed with dead leaves that had been crushed up.

By 2002 English people were drinking more coffee than tea anyway.

## English is ... wild words

Is the English language really as barbaric as the bishop claimed?

Yes, the English language has some ugly words like...

And some beautiful words...

Still, English is now spoken by a BILLION people round the world. So it can't be THAT bad.

Sadly, some great English words have fallen out of fashion. In fact you may not even know what they mean:

**1 Garbeller**
a) A toilet cleaner
b) A woman who talks too much
c) A food inspector

**2 Puttee**
a) A soldier's leg-guard in First World War
b) A game played by Henry VIII
c) Queen Victoria's three-legged goat

**3 Rafflesia**
a) A disease that made the ears drop off
b) A very smelly weed
c) Elizabeth I's pet dog

**4 Anhungry**
a) hungry
b) furious
c) ugly

**5 Hobbledehoy**
a) A villain who steals knickers
b) A woman who eats with her mouth open
c) A youth aged 14 to 21

**6 Moyled**
a) boiled in mustard
b) covered in mud
c) hanged by the thumbs

**7 Derrick**
a) A stupid boy
b) A post for executing criminals
c) A plague rat

**8 Obumbrated**
a) put in the shade
b) kicked up the bum
c) given a bump on the head by a brat

**9 Gyves**
a) herbs that make you throw up
b) spotted trousers worn by jesters
c) a torture machine

**10 Humpty-dumpty**
a) a drink made of boiled brandy and beer
b) a bad-tempered teacher
c) a big bad egg

179

*Answers:*

**1 c)** In the fifteenth century London grocers sent out garbellers to check that grocers weren't cheating the public. If a grocer DID sell spices mixed with sawdust then they were locked in a pillory and the spices burned under their noses.

**2 a)** In 1914 Britain went to war with Germany and the soldiers needed to wrap a bandage – a putti – round each trouser leg to keep the mud out. Sadly they didn't keep the bullets out.

THIS ONE'S HARDLY MUDDY AT ALL

**3 b)** The British traveller Sir Thomas Stamford Raffles discovered these plants around 1820 and named them after himself. But who wants to have a stinking weed named after them?

**4 a)** William Shakespeare used the word in the 1600s and it simply means 'hungry'. But it's a great quiz question: 'What three English words end with the letters n-g-r-y?' The answer? 'Hungry', 'angry' and ... there isn't another one, it's a trick question! Unless you count anhungry, of course.

**5 c)** A Tudor word for someone who is neither a man nor a boy. No one is quite sure where the word comes from but many *Horrible Histories* readers are hobbledehoys.

**6 b)** Before English roads were covered in tar they could turn very muddy in winter. Travellers ended up very moyled.

**7 b)** A hangman in the 1600s was called Mr Derrick and his grisly scaffold was named after him.

**8a)** The first great dictionary was written by Dr Samuel Johnson and he 'collected' this word that no one ever uses. But he was a failed schoolteacher so what else would you expect?

**9 c)** A clever torture machine like an iron ball – open it up, pop the victim in and close it till he is crushed – or tells you what you want to know. Used in the Tower of London.

**10 a)** Maybe it was drunk by all the king's horses and all the king's men. They were then too drunk to put the fat egg together again!

# Awful for animals

The English are famous for loving animals – they don't eat horses (unlike the foul French) or battle with bulls (like the savage Spanish) or dine on dogs (like the kruel Koreans). But England hasn't always been a happy home for animals...

## Catching cranes

The English have always enjoyed hunting. Saxon King Ethelbert II of Kent sent a message to the monk Boniface in Germany asking if he'd send some German goshawks back.

The hawks in kent are no good for hunting cranes. You sent me two falcons and a goshawk last year and I would be pleased if you could send me two more of the goshawks.

Elizabeth R

You don't see many cranes in England these days. Wonder why?

Of course, the king would tell you he wasn't cruel. He killed the cranes for food. But the truth is crane meat is a bit tough. It has to be allowed to rot for three days or so before it is cooked. Scrummy, eh?

## Pigeon pie

The Great Fire of London destroyed a large part of the city in 1666. But it wasn't just the people who were left homeless. Samuel Pepys kept a diary at that time and told of the city in cinders...

Went down to the Tower of London where the governor told me the fire began in the King's baking house in Pudding lane. I took a boat to see for myself. The poor people were trying to rescue their goods before the fire reached them, flinging them into the river. Many people stayed in their houses till the fire touched them then ran to the boats.

And among other things, the poor pigeons were not willing to leave their homes. They hovered around the windows and gutters till they burned their wings and fell to the ground.

## Miserable monkey

In the 1830s Jack Mytton was a rich (but stupid) Englishman. One of his favourite pets was a monkey that went out hunting on horseback with him. Mutt-head Mytton decided it would be a funny trick to teach his monkey to drink wine. The monkey enjoyed it and got a taste for it, but one day, desperate for a drink, he drank a bottle of boot polish ... and it polished him off.

*SHOE-BOOZE, SHOW-BIZ GEDDIT?

### Super for spiders

In Tudor England it was more fun being a spider. There's an old saying...

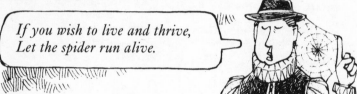

*If you wish to live and thrive, Let the spider run alive.*

The 'Cardinal Spider' was named after Henry VIII's friend Cardinal Wolsey. It was said to be wise and could heal you. (It was also hairy and over 12 cm long. If that dropped on you in the bath the shock could kill you!)

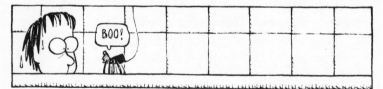

Henry VIII and his friends made the spiders special guests at their feasts. (Well, after all, spiders don't eat a lot of roast pork and Henry VIII didn't eat a lot of flies, so they made good pals.)

Cardinal Wolsey, meanwhile, upset Henry and was sent for trial and probably the chop. Wolsey did a very sensible thing and died before he could be executed.

## Horrible for hounds

James I loved to hunt and, from time to time, his wife Anne of Denmark joined him. Sadly Anne of Denmark was Anne Off-the-Mark when she shot an arrow at a deer – and killed the king's favourite hunting hound instead.

Oooops!

But James forgave her. As the dog was called 'Jewel' he gave her a jewel worth £2,000 and said the dog had left the jewel in its will.

## Grim for geese

It's rotten being an English goose. As well as being cooked and eaten you could be used as a tug boat!

William Cooke's circus used geese to pull Nelson the clown along a river in the 1840s. It was an advert for his circus.

When they reached Great Yarmouth (Norfolk) hundreds of people crowded on to the bridge to see the fun. The bridge collapsed. 130 people drowned.

Not the geese, though.

## Brutal for bulls

The English never went in for bullfighting, but they did enjoy setting their dogs to fight bulls in the 1700s and 1800s. Butchers said that the beef tasted better if a bull was angry when it was killed – making the bull furious with dogs turned into the 'sport'. It also led to the ancient *Horrible Histories* joke...

The aim was for the dog to grab the bull by the nose and hang on.

* The bull was tied up and a dog let into the ring.
* If the dog failed it could be tossed to death on the bull's horns.
* Another dog would be sent into the ring ... and another.
* If a dog 'won' then the bull was killed.

A popular day for this 'sport' was 21 December. It was finally banned in 1835. Why?

**a)** because young princess victoria said it was cruel
**b)** because men at bullrings got drunk and started fights
**c)** because england was getting short of bulls.

> *Answer:* **b)** The audience went a bit wild – like football hooligans today. The cruelty wasn't stopped because anyone felt sorry for the bull!

*Did you know...?*
The centre of Birmingham used to be a bullring and it is still called that today.

### Tossed toads

The first new moon in May was NOT a good time for toads in ancient times. That was the day when Toad Men arrived and told your fortune. They did this by tossing toad bones on to the ground and reading your future from the pattern they made. Maybe nonsense but there was still a Toad Fair at Stalbridge in Dorset in the early 1800s.

### Dread for dogs

The English love dogs. Er ... no.

When the First World War started, any German type of dog could be treated with terrible cruelty because England was at war with Germany – even though the dog was born in England and didn't know there was a war on. Dachshunds were kicked in the street and two were burned alive.

IS THAT WHY THEY CALL THEM 'SAUSAGE' DOGS?

German Shepherds were re-named 'Alsatians' to protect them. Nothing new there. The British royal family changed their name from the German 'Saxe-Coburg-Gotha' to 'Windsor' and never changed back.

### Suffering stag

The English love deer. Hunting them. Have a go yourself...

*You need:*
• A wild stag
• A pack of hunting hounds
• Hunters on horses

*To play:*
1 Find a stag.
2 Let the dogs chase it till they catch it and tear its throat out.
3 Hunters keep up with the chase so you can enjoy the kill.
4 Eat the dead stag.

WOOF WOOF WOOF WOOF WOOF WOOF WOOF

TALLY-HO TALLY-HO TALLY-HO TALLY-HO TALLY-HO TALLY-HO

Is finding a stag a problem? Never mind, you can keep them in a park and set one free when you are ready to hunt. Give the stag a start, though – a good old English 'sporting' chance.

But it can go a little wrong. In January 1820 the *Oxford County Chronicle* described one hunt…

On Tuesday 21st January a stag was turned out from Blenheim Park. It set off down the main road to Oxford. The stag and the chasing dogs made one of the most beautiful sights you can imagine. They were followed by a great number of well-known sportsmen who followed it up Oxford High Street as far as Brasenose College. Then, to the amazement of 100s of spectators, the stag ran into the chapel during a holy service. There it was killed without fuss by the eager dogs.

The chase had lasted over ten miles. Maybe the stag thought God would help him in that church.

What happens at the end of a stag hunt? A writer said…

*The beast did what most deer do: they find water, or a fence, or a wood, and they turn and face their hunters. At this point, the deer will be exhausted. It would rather turn and fight, or turn and die. But it cannot, or will not, go on running any longer.*

Of course that was written about a stag hunt in Somerset in the year 2000. Brand new century, same old killing. In 2004 it was finally made illegal to hunt stags with dogs.

**Dreadful Diary Day 12**
*28 February – Oswald's Day OR Sick Day*
This is the time when everyone needs a day off in memory of an old horse.

In AD 992 a strange and wonderful thing happened near Worcester. Oswald died by the side of the road. But don't worry! He was a great and good bishop so his death did a bit of good. Here's what happened later that year…

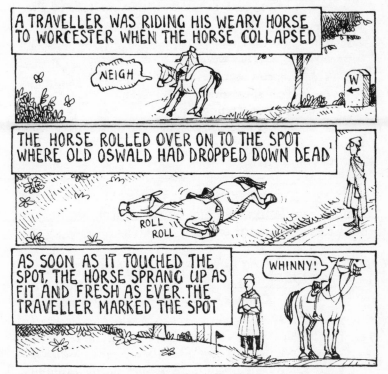

1 But luckily they'd moved old Ossie's body before the horse rolled there, otherwise they'd have had to bury him in a very wide, flat coffin.

That spot in Worcester is the source of healing and it's a pity we can't bottle it...

**28 FEB** **Celebrate this day:**
Everyone needs a day off today to go to Worcester and roll on the ground. If you are not feeling ill on that day then you will be by the time you've rolled around for a while on a foul February day.

# Epilogue

They're funny people, the English. You'd think they'd all join together and fight their enemies. But, no. They spend more time fighting each other ... and letting their enemies rule them.

Since the days of King Alfred they have been ruled by Vikings, then Norman French, then a Welsh family, then the Scots and finally, for the past 300 years, by a German family.

Most of all, the poor have fought against the posh – the working classes against the ruling classes. England became famous for its 'class wars'.

As the poor kept on struggling, they sang. In the 1830s the Chartists wrote their 'Anthem'. Many poor English people might still sing the Chartist Anthem today...

*A hundred years, a thousand years,*
*We're marching on the road.*
*The going isn't easy,*
*Yet we've got a heavy load.*
*The way is blind with blood and sweat,*
*And death sings in our ears.*
*But time is marching on our side:*
*We will defeat the years,*
*Oh we will defeat the years.*

Some people still think England is the best place in the world to live. They believe the horrible history is all in the past.

For some it is. For others 'the going isn't easy'. The rich still rule and the poor still suffer. But it's getting better and time is on the side of the rebels. One day they will defeat the years.

THEN CAN WE HAVE AN EXTRA DAY OFF?